English Language Project Work

Christine McDonald

MACMILLAN

First published 1992 by
THE MACMILLAN PRESS LTD
Houndmills, Basingstoke, Hampshire RG21 2XS
and London
Companies and representatives
throughout the world

ISBN 0–333–54117–0 hardcover
ISBN 0–333–54118–9 paperback

A catalogue record for this book is available
from the British Library.

Printed in Hong Kong

Reprinted 1994

Contents

Acknowledgements

In writing this book, I have been helped by many people and I should like to take this opportunity of thanking them.

Colleagues and students of Monkwearmouth College, Sunderland, have been of particular assistance. Thanks are due to Roger Brown and Vera Simpson for comments on earlier drafts, and to the many students who provided exemplar project work, in particular: Neil Barnes, David Boldon, Lynn Drinkald, Jánina Greenshields-Bell, Sharon Harper, Peter Houghton, Abbe Makinson, Andrew Mills, Joanne Hallett, Louise Pinkney and Kathryn Tutin.

Finally, the work would not have been possible without the support and encouragement of my husband, Ian, and the rest of my family.

The author and publishers wish to thank the following who have kindly given permission for the use of copyright material:

Bobby Thompson Record Co. for *The Little Waster*; Broad Laboratories, Slough, Berkshire, and the Metro Radio Group plc for the extract entitled *Dentrex Toothpaste*; R. H. Patterson & Co. Ltd for the extract entitled *Patterson's Showroom*; Air Canada, British Airways, British Midland, Dan Air, GKN Automotive AG and TWA for transcriptions of speech between air traffic controllers and pilots; the University of Oklahoma Press for the Chaucer facsimile from the Hengwrt manuscript, from *The Canterbury Tales* (ed. Paul G. Ruggiers, 1979).

Every effort has been made to trace all copyright-holders, but if any have been inadvertently overlooked the publishers will be pleased to make the necessary arrangement at the first opportunity.

List of cassette recordings

1
Introduction

Recent changes generally in A and AS examinations suggest that course work has a part to play at this level of study. In the English subject area, the introduction of new A and AS examinations in English Language has seen the appearance of a new element, knowledge about language, an area which is often unfamiliar for both teachers and students. In many syllabuses, more stress is also being placed on spoken English.

The aim of this book therefore is to provide a structured framework for tackling knowledge about language course work with special emphasis on spoken English. Such course work is usually based on the student's own data. Some time is therefore spent on the various methods of transcribing spoken material. The cassette tape which accompanies the book contains recordings of transcriptions given in Chapters 7 and 15 for projects based on spoken material.

The book is addressed to the student and should be useful for some of the more flexible approaches to learning which have appeared recently. Students following open learning, flexi-study, resource-based workshop, distance learning or correspondence courses will be able to use the material for independent or supported study. The book provides a step-by-step guide to tackling a language project. The various key stages could be discussed with larger groups of students and used as a springboard for individual work.

Such course work could contribute especially to the development of the core skills of communication and problem solving. In the course of their research work, students learn how to select and organise from the vast amount of information they amass in order to present a structured written report of their findings. The use of graphs, tables and charts requires some skill in numeracy. They also collect data, locate reference sources and are involved in individual and group discussion about their work.

Students develop personally by tackling a sustained piece of work independently. They learn to apply the skills of critical analysis to new material. Opportunities for the use of information technology arise particularly in the word processing of the final product. Such an English language component is also a good preparation for the study of other languages and could be used to reinforce any cross-curricular theme, depending on the content of the data chosen.

Although some language areas are explained in the book, it is assumed that students have some language background by the time they reach the project stage, which is usually more than half-way through the course. Exercises are provided at the end of most sections and chapters.

2

Planning a timetable

First of all, read the syllabus you are studying. This will ensure that you know exactly when the deadlines are and what the requirements are. Bear in mind that the deadlines for submission to the examination board or for moderation are likely to be several weeks after submission to your school or college, where projects may have to be marked or processed first. If your syllabus requires spoken material, you will know not to include or base your project on any written material. You also need to be aware of any word or tape limits, or any specifications about the sections to be included in your project.

There is a certain amount of preliminary work which needs to be done before you start on the actual write-up of your project – you need to take this into account when planning your timetable. During your course, you should have been thinking about and reading around the subjects that interest you with a view to choosing your area of study. You should try to have some idea of what you hope to prove. If your project involves any spoken material, you will already have practised recording and transcribing. If you are basing your project on written material, you will need to be on the look-out for interesting examples to collect. Once you have chosen your topic and collected your material, you need to clarify your aim. Next, you should ensure that your material is accurately presented by faithfully transcribing spoken material and using facsimiles (exact copies) of written material where possible. Having undertaken this preliminary work, you are now ready to start work in earnest on the actual data.

Once you start writing up the project, remember that much

3

of what you do at first is likely to be a rough draft which could have to be rewritten in the light of your findings. At this stage, you need to divide your work into manageable portions. It's useful to think of the project in terms of four sections, in addition to the material used as evidence:

1   An introduction to the subject containing an explanation of what is going to be studied and the method of investigation to be adopted.
2   A description of the material and the context or situation associated with it.
3   An analysis of the language with comment and explanation.
4   A conclusion or evaluation showing the insights you have gained.

Your project is meant to be original, so your analysis will probably take up most of the time. It's best therefore to divide your time further when undertaking the analysis so that you concentrate on one language aspect at a time. Finally, you need to allow time to rewrite and polish your final version before handing it in.

When planning the best time to start, you need to take into account the amount of work outlined so far. Obviously, the best time to start depends on the sort of person you are and the type of course you are following: one year, two year, full time, part time, open learning and so on. If you start too early, there are two main dangers: first, you will not have sufficient linguistic background to write competently; second, you will lose impetus by spreading your project over too long a period. On the other hand, there is a danger if you don't start work until the term before the deadline: you will need to be very self-disciplined, dividing your time wisely and putting in a concentrated effort, otherwise you will fail to finish the final polished version for submission on time. You also need to allow extra time in case some things go wrong. Don't forget to discount any time for mock examinations. Finally, remember that the deadline is an external one. Unlike the odd internal essay here or there which can be handed in late, this deadline is not subject to extension.

If your deadline for the submission of your project is the spring, then the best time to start writing up a project in earnest is by the Christmas of the previous year. In other words, you need to allow at least a good term before the deadline to write up your project. You may need to bring this forward if you have other course work commitments as well. You should also have ensured that preliminary work on reading, choosing and deciding on a rough aim, and collecting and transcribing material is completed before you start on the write-up.

A suggested timetable which shows the number of weeks of hard work required for your project is as follows:

A   From the beginning of the
    course
    BE ALERT   1   Be on the look-out for
                                  interesting and
                                  worthwhile topics.

    COLLECT   2   Practise recording and
                                  transcribing spoken
                                  material. Don't miss an
                                  opportunity of recording
                                  something which might be
                                  of use later.
                                      Collect any promising
                                  written material, if you
                                  are using written data.

    READ   3   Read around any topics
                                  you might tackle for your
                                  project. Long holidays are
                                  a good time for reading.

B   Two terms before the
    deadline
    CONSULT & DECIDE   4   Consult your teacher or
                                  lecturer and make a
                                  definite decision on your
                                  area of study. Devise a
                                  possible title.

THINK	5	Have some idea about your reasons for choosing the topic, and what you aim to discover and concentrate on.
RECORD & SELECT	6	Record and, if necessary, edit any tape extracts to about 3–5 minutes in length so that the whole recording contains interesting and significant features. Take care not to discard any edited material too early.
		Select any written extracts, if you are using written data.
TRANSCRIBE & COPY	7	Make an accurate spoken transcription in conventional spelling, thinking as you go along about the significant features and how you might organise them in your analysis. Add phonetic or prosodic features if necessary. Choose any bits which might be useful for an edited version with no non-fluency.
		Try to obtain facsimiles if you are using written data. Look over your material for possible interesting features to discuss.
READ	8	Draw up a reading list and do a book search for any

relevant background material or ideas. You should keep reading around the subject over the next few weeks.

C A term before the deadline

Week 1
DISCUSS
9 You should be discussing first drafts of any transcriptions and other sections of your project on a regular basis from now on. This is very important, otherwise you may go off in the wrong direction. You may need to alter first drafts as you go.

INTRODUCTION
10 Write a rough introduction, briefly reviewing the area and outlining your reasons, aims and methods.

Week 2
DESCRIPTION
11 Draft a description, explaining the context of the recorded or written material (who, where, when, what and how) and any other background information.

Week 3
DIVIDE
12 Check your transcription, if using spoken data, and decide roughly on the subsections of your analysis, which you can now begin. Sound, vocabulary, grammar, semantics and discourse structure are useful areas

to look at, but the subsections you eventually use will depend on your material. Look at it carefully before deciding.

Weeks 4–8 **ANALYSIS**	13	Spend about a week writing up a rough draft of each subsection of your analysis. This timetable assumes you have about five subsections, but if you have more, you need to work accordingly.
Week 9 **CONCLUSION**	14	Write a rough draft of your conclusion or evaluation.
Week 10 **CHECK**	15	Check your first version for length, style, expression, spelling, punctuation and so on. You may need to rewrite or polish certain sections. Sometimes the introduction needs to be rewritten in the light of what you have found.
Week 11 **POLISH**	16	Write, word process or type your final version, making it look attractive and presentable. A contents list and dividers may be needed.
Week 12 **CHECK & HAND IN**	17	Check your final version, hand it in, congratulate yourself and breathe a sigh of relief.

Exercise 1

After having read this suggested timetable, draw up a timetable for your own project, taking into consideration your personal circumstances and the requirements of your examination. Some examination boards require you to keep a log of your progress. If you need to do this, you should start to make notes from now on, on the processes and activities of your study.

3
Choosing a topic

When choosing a topic, make sure that it is the language that you are primarily interested in, not something which is, for instance, too generally sociological or too like literary criticism. The syllabus probably provides a list of suggested topics for you to consider. These are useful as a starting point to give you an idea of potential subjects, but there is a danger that everybody in the country who is entered for that examination will choose one of the few suggestions listed. Your examination board might provide a longer list of titles which have been tackled.

Before choosing a topic, you must obviously have some competence in the terminology used to describe language – this book assumes that you have some background knowledge. During your course, you will have come across symbols and terms used to describe many of the following: spoken English and conversation, the sounds of English, prosodics (for example, rhythm, volume, speed, pitch and so on), spelling and graphology, vocabulary, grammar and the semantics (meaning) of the language. You probably won't need terms and symbols from all of these areas; by now you should have some idea about which areas you feel most competent in, and you may like to focus on one or more of these.

For example, if you need to use spoken data and you are good at phonetics, you could look at your local accent. The speaker you choose could also have some dialect features, so you should be prepared to mention grammatical or vocabulary differences as well, if these occur. If you are not very good at spotting whether tones rise or fall in spoken material, you could avoid this by specifying in your introduction that you are concentrating on the segmental sounds (that is, the consonants and vowels) of the accent. This is easy if the accent doesn't have a very distinctive intonation pattern, or if you have enough to write about without mentioning intonation. If you do not feel confident with phonetic or grammatical terms but have intuitions about turn-taking and such like, you might like to base a spoken project on conversation. You could choose from a variety of situations, involving, for instance, table talk, arguments, radio discussions or even telephone conversations. The situations are potentially limitless. You need to make sure, however, that you write about the language and do not give just a narrative account.

Having discovered which areas you are best at, you need to choose a topic which will exploit your expertise, and which will be relevant and interesting to you. Most students choose topics which relate to careers or hobbies, or are also of some relevance to other subjects they are studying. You might want to study a variety of English which has not been discussed during your course, or to further your knowledge by an in-depth study of a familiar variety. Some examples of topics chosen by various students, along with their titles and reasons, are outlined below. The titles are divided into those suitable for spoken material, those suitable for written material and those suitable for either. Many titles can be adapted for material from another medium. There are a large number of projects in which spoken and written varieties could be contrasted. Care must be taken, however, not to make your area of study too large and unmanageable, especially if dealing with extracts from more than one source.

Spoken topics
1 *Airspeak* This was based on recordings between West Drayton air traffic control (ATC) and various aircraft. The student's hobby was plane spotting and career intentions were in ATC.
2 *The language of humour* This was based on the student's favourite comedy programme involving Lennie Henry.
3 *The language of a soap opera* This was based on an extract from 'Eastenders', a programme the student was

interested in. The student's intended career was in broad-casting. Theatre Studies was another of the A levels being studied.

4 *Sports commentary on local hospital radio* The student did voluntary work for the local hospital radio and was a keen supporter of the local football team.

5 *Motherese* The student had a young baby sister and monitored the way the baby's mother altered her language when talking to the baby. The student's career intentions were in nursery or infant education.

6 *Nigerian pidgin* The student had lived for some time in Nigeria and was interested in contrasting news bulletins in Standard English and the local pidgin.

7 *Male and female language* The student was an ardent feminist and wanted to see if there were any differences between the way six male and six female students gave directions from the college to the town centre bus station.

8 *CB radio language* The student was a keen CBer and recorded some local exchanges.

9 *The language of some students with learning difficulties and their teacher* The student's intended career was as a special needs teacher. The family had contacts with a local special needs centre. (This project can also be done with hard of hearing children, although transcription is difficult, especially if the children have been totally deaf from birth.)

10 *Political rhetoric* This project was based on the examination of the speech of some well-known orators: Winston Churchill, Martin Luther King and President Kennedy. The student was an active member of a political party and was also studying Government and Politics.

11 *The language of a chat show* The student was interested in Terry Wogan's ability as a host and analysed this in an interview with a guest.

12 *A radio phone-in* The techniques of a local DJ with an insulting manner were analysed.

13 *Teacher talk* The student intended to be a teacher and was interested in looking at teaching technique and control

in a short extract from a lesson. (With this title, it would also be possible to contrast the approach taken by various teachers for various age groups.)

14   *A contrast between two accents*   The student was upset that local speakers were often classified as Geordies when they came from the neighbouring area of Wearside. The student examined two short extracts from two speakers to show that there were differences between the two regions.

15   *Telephone techniques*   This was based on several short extracts involving telephone selling and answer phone machines. The student had been involved with telephone reception work on work experience and had access to telephone recording facilities.

16   *Time travel*   The student recorded four generations in a family (sister, mother, grandmother and great-grandmother), each talking about a holiday.

Written topics

1   *Chaucer's English*   Based on a written version of part of *The Canterbury Tales*. The student was also studying English Literature and History.

2   *Legal language*   The student's intended career was as a solicitor. Permission could not be obtained to record in the local courts, so the student had to be content with looking at written legal language in wills, contracts and such like. (For speech, a solicitor's edited dictaphone messages could have been used.)

3   *Newspeak*   This was based on a contrast between the treatment of an incident involving the hippies and Stonehenge in various newspapers: broadsheet, tabloid, national, local, weekly and an English version of a Russian newspaper. The student was interested in journalism as a career.

4   *Hopkins*   The student was studying English Literature and wanted to examine and evaluate Hopkins's style in some poems. (In similar projects, the style of any author could be examined, or a contrast could be made between different authors writing on the same topic.)

Spoken and written topics

1 *The language of a seven-year-old*   This was based on a conversation and some reading with a pupil, and on the pupil's written work. The student was involved in work experience in a primary school and wanted to be a primary school teacher in the future.

2 *Franglish*   The student was studying French, had been involved in several exchange visits and wanted to become an EFL (English as a Foreign Language) teacher. A French pen-friend was recorded speaking English and the letters received were also examined for difficulties with English.

3 *Advertising language*   The student's intended career was in advertising. Persuasive techniques in advertising in a variety of media were examined. The student was also studying Communication Studies, in which advertising was a part of the syllabus.

4 *The language of religion*   The student examined both spoken and written religious language. Written extracts were taken from the Bible, from hymns and from the Prayer Book. The student's father, who was a vicar, was willing to be recorded, and so extracts from his sermon were also used.

5 *A study in story-telling*   The student recorded the well-known local story-teller in the local pub and contrasted his narrative techniques with a written version of the story.

6 *Parliamentary debate*   This was based on exchanges in the House of Commons. A contrast was made between the spoken version and the written record in Hansard. The student had political ambitions and wanted eventually to become an MP.

7 *Style*   This was based on the varieties used by one speaker as she conversed with her husband, young daughter and dog, and in written forms such as notes and personal and business letters.

The possibilities for topics are limitless. You could focus on the user of the language, choosing age, gender, region, education, social class or such like as the focus, or you could concentrate on the use of language, bearing in mind, for example, whether

a monologue or a dialogue is involved, which context or
situation the language occurs in, and what the purpose is. I'm
sure you can think of many more topics of interest and
relevance to you. Chapters 4 and 15 (which contains completed
projects) have further examples and ideas. Before deciding on
your topic, it might be worthwhile reading these.

4

Variations on a theme

Even if you choose a topic similar to others in your group, it is still possible to look at yours from a different angle. This chapter gives some suggestions for variations on a theme.

4.1 Accents and dialects

The local accent and dialect is an obvious choice for study as you will have intuitions about this that many outsiders don't have. However, if you have moved around the country or have parents from a different region, you may prefer to study an accent other than that of the region you are currently living in. One possibility is to examine how far the influence of a different area can be detected in the speech of one speaker, although this is difficult and demands a good phonetic knowledge.

The varieties available involve not only rural and urban accents and dialects in England (for example, West Country, Northumbrian, Newcastle, Birmingham, Liverpool, London and so on), but also varieties spoken elsewhere in Britain (Scots, Welsh, Irish) and other national varieties of English (American, Australian, Indian, various creoles and so on).

Received Pronunciation (RP) has been well studied but there are possibilities even here. If you have recordings of RP from 50 years ago and contrast these with conservative and advanced types of RP spoken today, you will notice some differences which indicate that RP is not always the same (for example, *poor* as /puə/ or /pɔ:/, *off* as /ɒf/ or /ɔ:f/). Again, however, this

16

topic is difficult and may not provide enough features for a long project, unless you judiciously edit or are lucky with the features in your material, and unless your syllabus allows you to include quite a bit of general material on the development of RP. Usually, however, examination boards prefer your project to be mainly original research, not just regurgitation of general background information.

If your examination board allows you to include written material, you might want to study regional use in some local dialect poems or short stories. Sometimes such writing is humorous because of a mismatch between the situation and the dialect. Often, parodies (imitations) of Standard English forms are involved.

Contrasting accent by age, sex or class is another possibility, although here you must make sure that, as far as possible, all other variables are constant. For example, when contrasting the speech of men and women, you should ensure that they are of a similar age and class, and come from the same region. If contrasting middle and working class speakers in your area, you should try to ensure that they are of a similar age – you may even want to concentrate on either males or females. You should also make sure that the situations in which the recordings are made are of a similar formality. These studies could all involve quite small differences in pronunciation, so you would need to be good at phonetics to undertake such projects.

A study of dialect features generally involves more editing than a study of accent features, as particular sounds occur more frequently than particular grammatical features. Only a few of the grammatical features that you are interested in will occur in any given 3–5 minutes of continuous speech, so you could have to make up your tape from several short extracts, although you must be careful not to make it sound too disjointed. You might even have to resort to structuring an interview to elicit the sorts of features that you are interested in. When studying pronunciation, you could use prepared passages of reading material and word lists to ensure that the features under study occur. The tape accompanying the Hughes and Trudgill (1979) book, *English Accents and Dialects*, has examples of word lists, as well as spontaneous speech from various parts of the country.

However, prepared passages and word lists are often artificial and could be less interesting for your project than spontaneous speech.

4.2   Child language

A large number of different projects can be undertaken on child language; for example:

1   The pronunciation of a relatively young baby.
2   The lexical and grammatical acquisition of a pre-school child.
3   The social use of language at a later stage.
4   The degree of adult competence in an older child or children.
5   A contrast between two children of the same age to show their varying degrees of acquisition at one or more levels (pronunciation, vocabulary, grammar and even social use).
6   A study of one child to see how far acquisition corresponds with the expected order suggested in textbooks on the subject.
7   A developmental study of one child over a short period of time.
8   Adult usage to children, often called 'caretaker speech'.
9   An examination of children's writing to see how far they have written in Standard spelling and dialect with a view to explaining the concepts they have still to grasp.
10   A contrast between the everyday speech of a child and the reading material in school.
11   An examination of school reading material from various subjects or for various ages.

Whichever project you choose, make sure that it has a suitable title which is different from anyone else's in your group. It would be no good calling all the above projects 'Child language'. One project might be called 'The pronunciation of a two-year-old', another 'The vocabulary and grammar of a pre-school child', and yet another 'Social use and language mastery in primary school children'. Other titles could include 'Child language development', 'Children's reading and writing', 'Caretaker speech', 'Motherese' and so on.

4.3 Sports commentary

There are also several different approaches which can be taken to sports commentary. The following are possibilities:

1 A contrast between the commentaries for different sports (for example, football, swimming, tennis, cricket, squash and so on).
2 A contrast between local and national commentaries, especially for point of view and suitability to the audience.
3 A contrast between television and radio commentaries or newspaper reports of the same event to see how the medium affects the language.
4 An examination of the expertise of the reporter or commentator showing, for example, the various strategies for avoiding non-fluency in unscripted speech or commenting on the written style.

Whichever topic you choose, there will be many different ways of approaching it. It is up to you to decide on your approach, so that you know what sort of material to look for. However, bear in mind that if everyone in your school or college chooses the same topic, this can be fairly dull for the examiner.

Exercise 1

Before proceeding, jot down one or more possible topics of interest to you and then try to make a definite decision on your area of study.

5

Deciding on an aim

You could form a hypothesis about your chosen subject from various books on the topic. On the other hand, if there is little written on the subject that you have chosen, or you are interested in finding out about what appears to be an unknown area, you may have to form your theory or theories from personal observation. Ideally, you need to have some aim in mind before you choose your area of study. An aim will mean that you are in a much better position to choose suitable material, as you will have an idea, however vague initially, of what you are looking for, or of what you are trying to prove or disprove.

However, your aim could change as you examine your material – additional or different ideas may come to you. This shouldn't worry you: it means you are responding to the material in hand, not to some preconceived ideas. Good choice of material with plenty of relevant and interesting features is the basis of a good project, so you need to know what you are looking for from the outset. If you have ideas on specific areas that you think you'll need to focus on, you should jot these down alongside your aims. The areas may change and will become more specific as you start transcribing and looking at your material in detail.

Some examples of typical preliminary aims and a focus for the topics already mentioned in Chapter 3 are given below.

Spoken topics
1 *Airspeak* To characterise the language of ATC, as I am

not aware that this has been done before. To discover if language 'misuse' could contribute to 'near misses' in view of the increasing number of these recently. I think I'll need to look at dialogue features, pronunciation, vocabulary and grammar.

2 *The language of humour* To find out exactly what makes the comedy tick linguistically. I think prosodics and semantics will come into the project, as well as accent and vocabulary and possibly grammar.

3 *The language of a soap opera* To see how far scripted dialogue is like unscripted conversation. To see if each character is associated with typical language uses. I intend to focus on non-fluency and turn-taking. I'll also concentrate on the cockney and colloquial pronunciation, vocabulary and grammar.

4 *Sports commentary on local hospital radio* To ascertain how professional these commentators are. (They don't like to be called amateurs.) To see if the audience affects the commentary. I'll need to look at prosodics, fluency features, point of view and possibly other features associated with commentaries.

5 *Motherese* To look at ways in which a mother might or might not encourage her child's language acquisition. I'm not sure of exact headings, but I'll need to look at speed, pitch, pausing, simplified speech sounds, vocabulary and grammar, repetition, expansion and correction.

6 *Nigerian pidgin* To begin to write a grammar of Nigerian pidgin, including characterising the sounds of the language. To see where the various features might have come from. I'll have to investigate the pronunciation, where the vocabulary comes from and the typical features of the grammar.

7 *Male and female language* To see if there are indeed differences between the sexes, as textbooks differ on this matter. To evaluate which method of giving directions is the best, if there are any differences. Prosodics, paralinguistics and fluency features are likely to be important. I'll also look at the grammar (standard versus non-standard) and the pronunciation (RP versus local accent). Tag

questions and intensifiers may figure. Vocabulary might be worth looking at.

8 *CB radio language*   To characterise the language of CB, as I am unaware of other works on the subject. To explain what is often a 'closed' book to the uninitiated. I'll probably go through and pick out individual phrases and expressions and explain and comment on them. Turn-taking might also be important.

9 *The language of some students with learning difficulties and their teacher*   To find out if there are similarities between these youths and what we would expect from younger, normal children. To examine the way in which the teacher encourages their language learning. I imagine pronunciation, vocabulary and grammar will be like younger children's, while the teacher might use the language techniques of both a parent and a teacher.

10 *Political rhetoric*   To see which persuasive and rhetorical methods are used by the speakers. Prosodics is likely to play some part in the speeches, but I'll need to look for other features of language patterning as well.

11 *The language of a chat show*   To examine how skilful (or otherwise) a chat show host is in controlling the discourse, and in conversational and other language skills. I'll have to see how far I think the programme is scripted and analyse the conversation features. I'm not sure what else at the moment.

12 *A radio phone-in*   To characterise the speech of a well-known local DJ and to try to discover why people keep phoning in to be insulted. There could be some differences between the accent, dialect and fluency of the DJ and that of the people phoning in. The DJ might have intonation patterns showing attitudes like sarcasm. Loaded vocabulary items and taboo subjects might be worth looking at, as might turn-taking. I'll try to evaluate the programme at the end.

13 *Teacher talk*   To discover some hints for good teaching technique (or otherwise). I'll need to look at structures used in passing on information, encouraging, correcting, reprimanding, criticising, consulting and so on.

14 *A contrast between two accents* To show, using a vowel chart, that there are indeed differences between the two accents I am studying. I don't think anyone has described my local accent before. To contrast the accents with RP and suggest some reasons for the differences. I'll look at vowels (monophthongs and diphthongs) and consonants and try to organise them into some sort of system. I also intend to mention something about attitudes to accents. If any dialectal features occur, I may have to mention these as well.

15 *Telephone techniques* To establish any differences from face-to-face conversation. Paralinguistics, fluency and turn-taking could be important. To evaluate answer phone messages. The style may be different here. To identify if there is a strategy in telephone selling, so that I am better able to cope with it. Loaded questions might play an important part here. I might have too much to cope with overall, so I might have to focus on only one of these aims when I record my material.

16 *Time travel* To see if there are any age differences between the language used by the four generations. This will give me apparent as opposed to real time differences in language use. It isn't going to be easy, so I might have to abandon this project in favour of something else if I can't find enough features in my material. I'll be looking for any older pronunciations, vocabulary items and syntax. Speed, fluency and differences in formality might also be important.

Written topics
1 *Chaucer's English* To help me understand his language better, so that I will develop a greater appreciation of the literary and historical features associated with it. At the moment, I think I'll need to look at the change in spelling, vocabulary and grammar over time. The sources of the vocabulary could be important. The spelling might also give a clue as to possible pronunciation.

2 *Legal language* To discover exactly what sort of language is used in legal documents. I would expect punctuation,

s and grammar to be very distinctive in this occupational
of language.

3   *Newspeak*   I'll look at content, selection of detail, point of
view, structure, positioning of items, vocabulary and style in
all of the different articles that I have collected on my
chosen topic. I would like to evaluate these for bias, skill in
reporting and suitability for intended audience.

4   *Hopkins*   To take a sample of Gerard Manley Hopkins's
poems and, using the techniques of analysis for looking at
literature, to come up with some features typical of Hopkins's style. I might be able to use a computer to collect data
on various features, which should save me some time.

Spoken and written topics

1   *The language of a seven-year-old*   To contrast the spontaneous spoken English of a seven-year-old with the English
used in reading and writing with a view to helping the child
to improve. I'll need to look at fluency and pronunciation
and probably some dialect and childish features. Spelling
and layout could be important in the reading text. There
may be more, but I'll have to wait and see.

2   *Franglish*   To discover which features of the native speaker
carry over into spoken and written English, so that I can
explain how to avoid mistakes. I know accent, intonation,
sentence structure, word order, prepositions and verbs are
important, but I'll have to organise them into categories. I
may find other areas are also important.

3   *Advertising language*   To make myself aware of the persuasive devices used in advertising. Voice quality and prosodics
will be important in the radio and television extracts;
layout, punctuation and spelling in the written extracts. I
also intend to look at vocabulary, grammatical patterning
and any other devices for attracting attention.

4   *The language of religion*   To characterise this variety and
to discover if it is indeed only one variety of English. Each
extract might have different vocabulary and grammar.
Some parts are likely to be based more heavily on the
written medium and others on the spoken medium.

5   *A study in story-telling*   To analyse the story-teller's narra-

tive technique and to discover what makes him and the story so entertaining. I'll look at if and how the spoken features are captured in the written version. I think I'll look at the beginning, the build-up, the punch-line and the end of each anecdote for language features. I'll need to look for monitoring of the audience and narrative syntax. I'll probably find some accent and dialect features. Speed, pausing and rhythm are likely to be important in the spoken version.

6 *Parliamentary debate*   To see what is typical of this sort of language and whether it is controlled or not. Turn-taking, vocabulary and grammar are likely to be important. Rhetorical devices may be used. Speed, volume and other prosodics will probably be worth looking at in the spoken material. I want to see how far the written record is an exact replica of the actual speech and if anything is lost in the written transcription.

7 *Style*   To show that we all change the way we speak and write according to circumstances, even in everyday situations. I'll examine all levels in my language analysis to see what I come up with.

Exercise 1

Before proceeding, write a paragraph about your chosen project, giving your reasons for your choice and your rough aims. You might also have some idea of what features you are going to look at initially. Add any such comments to your paragraph.

6

Collecting data

If your project involves written material, the collection of data should not prove too much of a problem. Most students have access to a photocopier and, provided that the material is not too bulky and does not present copyright difficulties, should manage to obtain exact copies where necessary. You may have to write to a copyright holder for permission to use material. Many people are perfectly amenable if you are using small amounts for educational purposes. If you are looking for original handwritten copies or early printed versions of texts, local libraries are usually helpful. For a small amount, often not much more than the cost of a stamp or a photocopy, they can obtain material for you from inter-library loans. Exact copies are particularly important if you are dealing with written material such as children's writing, newspapers, advertising and historical documents, where layout and spelling are likely to play a part. Remember that, in general, a thorough analysis of a small amount of material works better than a skimpy treatment of a large amount of material.

The recording of spoken material is likely to be less familiar to students. The rest of this section therefore deals with the recording of spoken material. If your project involves written material only, you may like to pass on to Chapter 8.

If your project involves recorded material, it is probably wise to start experimenting with the recording before the second last term. You could find that technical or other problems prevent you from achieving an acceptable recording first time. A cursory glance at your first recording may show that there aren't enough features to study. You can then change your mind about the topic or decide to rerecord in a different situation which will bring out the features that you are interested in. Take care, however, that you do not end up being indecisive, trying several topics in a row and finally doing one in a rush. Whatever you choose, there will be something interesting to say about it, provided you know the right place to look.

Time is also needed if you have to edit your recording to an acceptable length. Three to five minutes is the length suggested by one examination board: you should find plenty to say about a recording of this size provided that you choose it wisely. Transcriptions of recordings much larger than this prove to be mammoth tasks. The original recording could involve 30 or more minutes of speech, but much of this recording will be redundant, as the same features will crop up again and again. Beware of the danger of having too much material. Remember that it is much better to concentrate on a small amount and analyse it thoroughly. However, make sure that you have at least the minimum amount of recorded material suggested by your examination board, otherwise your analysis will be too thin.

Obviously, if you are going to study a topic such as development in the language acquisition of a child, this will also take time. Recordings will have to be made at intervals of several weeks or even months. Earlier during the course, an opportunity of making a recording for a potential project might have arisen – this shouldn't be missed.

Beware of discarding material too quickly, as usually there are more interesting features present in a recording than a first glance suggests. There is always the danger of discarding something which later you discover could have been useful. The golden rules are: don't edit your material until you are sure of its usefulness, take care not to edit the material you are actually using, and keep a spare copy in case of accidents or loss.

You should already have gained some familiarity with taping methods during your course. You will probably have learnt that, if you are making your own recording, it's not always easy to make it natural when people are aware of being taped. This is known as the 'observer's paradox'. To find out about language use, you have to observe it actually being used. However, as soon as you start observing either yourself or others, usage tends to become artificial. You could of course record surreptitiously (that is, without telling anyone), but this is not really ethical – you should try to obtain permission afterwards, if not beforehand. With time, however, people do become accustomed to the presence of a cassette player and occasionally forget that it is there.

It has been discovered that informants (the people whose speech you are studying) are more natural if they are talking about something they feel strongly about or are very interested in. If they discuss something exciting or dangerous that has happened to them, or memories of childhood and such like, the focus is taken away from the way they are actually speaking and their speech tends to be more natural. You might like to bear this in mind if it fits in with your aims. If the idea is just to get the informants talking, then research about their background and hobbies will pay off. A set of informal questions prepared in advance is likely to get them talking.

If you are recording your own material, you will need to think carefully about how you are going to set it up. Spontaneous speech might be sufficient for your purposes, but if it is not, you will need to devise a suitable situation. With child language, for example, you could use picture books and get the child to tell a story suggested by the pictures.

With practice, you will learn which is the best type of cassette player for you. You will also learn the best position for the cassette player: how close it or the microphone has to be for a good recording, where to place it to avoid background noise and vibration, or whether a good recording can be obtained if it is hidden. You will also find out whether it is best to record with the volume down, in order to minimise feedback from the speakers, and in which positions the other controls need to be placed. You should aim for the best quality possible, although it is unlikely that you will reach professional standards – this is nothing to worry about as long as the spoken material is audible and decipherable. It is quite usual in spontaneous speech, especially conversations involving a number of speakers, to be unable to hear the odd word or two.

If you are recording from the television or radio, or from a record or cassette, you will have fewer problems and the quality may be better. The material, however, will probably feel less personal and you will have learnt less about recording techniques.

Exercise 1

Before collecting your data, think about the material you will need to fulfil the aims you wrote about roughly in the last chapter. Write a paragraph about where the material is going to come from, who the writers or speakers are going to be, what it is going to be about, and when and how you are going to record it, if it is spoken material. Then record and edit your material to a suitable length, if it is spoken, or collect your material, if it is written. Your teacher or lecturer might want to listen to your tape or look at your written data at this stage to check that you have made a satisfactory choice of material. You might want to adopt the same procedure after the completion of each stage. You will probably benefit from discussion and guidance after rough drafts of any transcription, introduction, description, analysis and evaluation.

7
Transcription

A transcription is a written copy of speech. If you are studying written material, you will not need to write this out again if you have a facsimile (an exact copy) of the original material. You may, however, need to copy your written material accurately and neatly if a facsimile is not necessary or possible. Obviously, if you are producing your own writing for analysis, then this is a case when you will need to write it out. You might also need to do some copying out if you want to use edited extracts of your material to comment on. With spoken material, however, you will need to copy or transcribe your material from the spoken to the written form in order to study it. For many students, this is a new area of study. The first section therefore goes into some detail about how to do various types of transcription. It begins with an outline of a straightforward method of transcription using ordinary spelling, firstly dealing with a monologue and then looking at conversation (Section 7.2). The punctuation conventions used for speech are different from those used for writing and these become more complicated when more than one speaker is involved. The following section shows how prosodic features such as speed, stress and tone can be added to a transcription, if necessary. The final section looks at how to transcribe phonetically to show pronunciation, if this is needed. If your material involves only written data, you might want to skim read this chapter on transcription and move on to Chapter 8.

It is essential to have an accurate copy of what has been said. If you omit anything from the recording or add anything which is not there, then your analysis and commentary cannot be accurate, as it has been based on an inaccurate transcription.

This will call into question the validity of your whole project.

There is some academic merit in being able to do a full prosodic and phonetic transcription of your material, but as this is not easy, there is a danger that you could go sadly wrong. It is more practical to add prosodic and phonetic features selectively only if these are significant to your purpose, otherwise you will lose sight of the important features in a mass of less important detail. Thus, you do not need to do a prosodic and phonetic transcription of your recording alongside a conventional one if, for example, the direction of tones is not important or you are not studying the pronunciation of sounds. It is unwise to spend weeks or even months replaying your tape and puzzling over whether a tone is rising or falling or a combination of both, and capturing the exact phonetic value of each sound. You only need to make a prosodic and phonetic transcription if these are important to the variety of English being examined, if you have noted these as aims, and if you are going to mention them in your commentary. Even then, it might be possible to pick out only a small extract for such a detailed analysis, or use selected items throughout the recording. You need to use your common sense to gauge how far you need a detailed prosodic and phonetic transcription of the whole recording.

It should be clear by now that the type of transcription you do depends on your purpose. You should have come across various types of transcription throughout your course. These are dealt with now.

7.1 Spoken English

The major problem when students transcribe spoken English is that they use the same conventions as for written English. They put in full stops, capital letters and commas. This is extremely impractical, as in spoken English it is not always clear where a sentence ends, and pauses often occur in the middle of phrases or clauses where no punctuation would occur in writing. Thus, the transcription will be inaccurate. It will also prevent you from making important comments which might arise out of the pausing.

When transcribing spoken English, you can continue to use apostrophes for omission and possession, and capital letters can be used for proper nouns, although not for the beginning of sentences, even supposing you can identify these. Question and exclamation marks can be used where absolutely necessary for ease, although questions are usually indicated by word order and sometimes by rising intonation, while a loud voice for an exclamation can be marked in the margin. The section on prosodic transcription explains how to do this. Standard English orthography (spelling) or some form of conventional spelling should generally be used as far as possible, with pronunciation differences being shown underneath by the phonetic alphabet. It is not always clear how words should be pronounced if an attempt is made at showing this in normal orthography, unless there are accepted conventions for doing so. Dialect words should be spelt the best way that you can with some idea given of their pronunciation underneath.

In summary, do not use unconventional spelling, full stops, commas or capital letters for the beginning of sentences when transcribing spoken English.

Pauses must be marked. There are several current ways of doing this. A popular way is outlined here. Micropauses (pauses under a second) are marked wherever they occur, even if in the middle of structures, by a full stop inside round brackets (.). Sometimes micropauses are so short that they are easy to overlook. You must take care not to miss them. Any pause longer than a second is timed (timed pause), with the time in seconds written inside the round brackets. For example, (2.0) indicates a pause of 2 seconds. The length of a pause is sometimes significant. Some linguists use dashes to indicate the length of a pause. For instance, (–) indicates a pause of 1 second, (– –) a pause of 2 seconds and so on. Sometimes a pause is accompanied by an intake of breath. This is indicated by (.h). Unless your recording is very good, you will have to listen very hard for these – sometimes you will be unable to hear them.

A further mistake which students make when transcribing spoken English is the omission of non-fluency features. You must include all false starts, hesitations, recycling, pause fillers, repetitions, self-corrections and so on. It is sometimes appropriate to include extracts of the transcription from which all these non-fluency features have been edited, but the original transcription must include all of them.

The terms used for non-fluency features are a bit confusing in that different linguists (people who study language) define them in different ways and sometimes they have a different meaning in ordinary language use. This is something which you will have to get used to as it is fairly common in language study. You might find it useful to stick to the following definitions. If you define your terms and use them consistently, then there should not be a problem.

Non-fluent pausing occurs in the middle of a structure where no punctuation would occur in writing: 'it's Southall's er (.) goal kick'. Pausing can also be non-fluent if there are no pauses where punctuation would normally occur in writing: 'there is a free kick against Viv Anderson Everton don't like that decision'. Some people call non-fluent pauses hesitations.

Pause fillers are one of the ways of filling what could be an embarrassing silence with extra words. These filler words also prevent the hearer from thinking that the speaker has finished speaking. The term is confined to words such as *well*, *sort of* and *like*. These do have functions, such as helping to start an utterance (initiators like *well*), making the speaker sound less pedantic (softeners like *sort of*), and indicating the end of an utterance (for example, *like* in some parts of the country). However, they are in addition to the main meaning of the utterance and are usually thought of as fairly meaningless.

Hesitations are sounds which aren't words which are used to fill pauses. In Britain, these sounds tend to be represented by *er*, *erm* and *em*.

False starts occur when an utterance is started in one way, is unfinished and then completely abandoned for another structure: 'my Mum won't (.) well we want . . .'.

Repetition in this context is unintentional and involves the repetition of identical words and structures next to each other: 'her pillow is her pillow'.

Recycling is similar to repetition but involves a hitch in production where the initial sound(s) of a word are repeated before the speaker manages to get the word out. It is quite normal for this to happen on occasion; it is not a kind of stammering and stuttering: 'th. the hairs'.

Self-corrections are where the speaker realises that he/she has made a mistake and corrects it: 'you've got to get the stirrups and (.) I mean the girth'.

As these non-fluency features overlap, they are not always easy to tell apart. They occur quite normally because of the complicated process of spontaneous speech in which the speaker is planning ahead, checking back over what has been said, actually producing the sounds and monitoring the hearer, all at the same time.

A further convention when transcribing speech is the use of a full stop to indicate an unfinished word, as in *alw.* for *always.* Some linguists use a dash rather than a dot for this.

It is not unusual to be unable in parts to decipher what is being said, especially if you weren't there when the recording was made. The recordings on the cassette tape accompanying this book have been mainly taken from student projects and were not recorded professionally. This will give you some idea of the quality which is acceptable in project work. You must be frank if you cannot decipher parts of your own recording. It is best to use square brackets [ ] to enclose any bits that you are doubtful about. You may want to guess at the words or the possible number of words or syllables. If you can't do this, then a phonetic transcription might help. This is particularly useful for any foreign or unusual words which you can hear but are unsure of their spelling. More frequently, you will be able only to give the amount of time of unclear speech, although in the case of small amounts of time you will not even be able to do this. The options are as follows:

[?one Saturday]	You think that the speaker said 'one Saturday' but you are uncertain about it.
[?2 words]	You think that you can hear two words but you don't know what they are.
[?4 syllables]	You think that you can hear four syllables but they are unclear.
[?/wɒnsarədə/]	You might manage an approximate phonetic transcription but be unable to decipher the words.
[2 seconds unclear speech]	The amount of time is more than a second but the speech is too garbled to understand.
[unclear speech]	The amount of time is under a second.

Whatever system you use, you need to indicate your conventions in a key at the beginning of the transcription.

It is useful to have a cassette player which has a button which will keep replaying the same bit of tape, so that you can decide exactly what is being said and where the pauses and non-fluency features are. However, rewinding and replaying short sections will do equally well, although it is more laborious. Keep replaying short sections until you are certain about what you hear and have written it down accurately.

Layout, which is relevant to all transcriptions, must be clear. Again, there are various ways of doing this. A popular way is shown in the following extract from a project involving a student's own unprepared speech (cassette recording 1 (CR1) on the tape accompanying this book).

Transcription of a spontaneous monologue (CR1)

Key
(.)   – micropause under a second
(.h)   – pause accompanied by an intake of breath

(1.0) – timed pause, with the time in seconds written in
round brackets
w. – full stop indicates unfinished word
[?'ve] – square brackets show unclear speech
PH – initials of the speaker
Tape no. – tape counter number

Tape no.	Line no.	Speaker	
003	1	PH	[?wey] I[?'ve] lived at
	2		Washington all my life like erm
	3		(.) at four different places (.h) I
	4		lived at Concord to start w. (.)
	5		start with (.) then I moved to
	6		Barmston (.h) and then back
007	7		(.) then to Biddick (.) then to
	8		Columbia (.) and then back
	9		Con. er (1.0) back to Concord
	10		again . . .

The speaker needs to be listed in the margin in some way. You could name the speakers in the key, but if they wanted to remain anonymous, you could either use just their initials or give them letters of the alphabet: A, B, C, D and so on. Line numbers make it easy to refer to your transcription in the analysis. In addition, the examiner should not have to hunt around to find out what you are discussing. The tape counter number is not essential, as each cassette player will display a slightly different number, but it will make it easier for you to find the approximate place of what you are studying on the tape, especially if you are using the same cassette player all the time.

This transcription of a spontaneous monologue contains most of the features typical of a recording of unplanned speech: an unclear part (*'ve*), a pause filler (*like*), a hesitation (*erm*), an unfinished word (*w.*), unintentional repetition (*start w. start with*), non-fluent pausing (*Con. er (1.0) back to Concord*) and self-correction (*back Con. er (1.0) back <u>to</u> Concord again*), as well as the typical spoken structure of utterances with the use of *and then*, which allows the speaker to continue and which creates lengthy sections within the speech. *wey* is a dialect spelling of a word equivalent to Standard English *well*.

An edited version of this monologue in normal orthography, which is useful if you want to study the grammatical structure free from non-fluency features, might look as follows:

Edited version of spontaneous monologue
I've lived at Washington all my life at four different places. I lived at Concord to start with. Then I moved to Barmston, then to Biddick, then to Columbia and then back to Concord again.

If you want to study something for which no symbols exist, you might need to design some of your own conventions. An example of an invented convention which a student designed in order to study fluency in a football commentary can be seen in the following:

Transcription of a football commentary with an invented convention (CR2)

Key
underlining – denotes where there probably would have been a punctuation mark, indicating some kind of pause if the material had been written

Tape no.	*Line no.*	*Speaker*	
011	1	A	[?it's] Southall's er (.) goal kick
	2		(1.0) headed on by Pointon
	3		____ but there is a free kick (.)
013	4		against Viv Anderson ____
	5		Everton don't like that
	6		decision . . .

As mentioned earlier, you must be careful not to judge spoken English by the conventions of written English, as they are different media with different uses. However, the conventions can be used sparingly here to show the degree of fluency in the opening of the recording. The first and third pauses wouldn't be indicated in writing, while there are two places (at the beginning of line 3 and at the end of line 4) where a pause might be indicated in writing but the commentator doesn't stop. The only really fluent pause is the second one which occurs at the end of a minor sentence, although punctuation might not occur before *but* in writing.

A short transcription of one speaker written in conventional spelling will look something like the first transcription of a spontaneous monologue. If you are using spoken material, you will need to have such a transcription as a basic starting point. If your project has more than one speaker, however, then you will need more complicated conventions. These are dealt with in the next section.

Exercise 1

If your recording involves only one speaker, transcribe it using the conventions suggested, making sure that the transcription is accurate. As you are transcribing, note any significant language features, so that you can examine these later.

7.2   Conversation

Your transcription may not require anything more difficult than that described in the previous section, but if you have more than one speaker, the transcription will be more complicated. One of the problems of transcribing conversations is what happens when a second speaker takes a turn. Speaker B might wait until Speaker A pauses at the end of what is being said. Speaker B might then take an in-breath and begin a turn. This can be diagrammatically indicated as follows, where dashes denote speech:

Diagram of sequential speech (1)

Tape no.	Line no.	Speaker	
001	1	A	–––––––––––––––––––––
	2		–––––––––(.)
	3	B	(.h)––––––––
	4		–––––––––––––––––––––

Speaker A finishes speaking half-way along line 2. Speaker B starts a turn almost immediately half-way along line 3. (Speaker B does not start at the beginning of line 3 unless Speaker A continues to the end of line 2, as this might indicate that Speaker B is overlapping with Speaker A as Speaker A says the first half of line 2.)

If Speaker B had spoken for only a short time, the transcription would have looked like this:

Diagram of sequential speech (2)

Tape no.	Line no.	Speaker	
001	1	A	–––––(.)
	2	B	(.h)––––(.)
	3	A	(.h)–––
	4		–––––––––––––––––––––

Some people, however, prefer to put short interruptions in round brackets as follows:

Diagram of sequential speech (3)

Tape no.	Line no.	Speaker	
001	1	A	––––––––––––––––––––––––
	2		–––––(B: yeah) –––––––––
	3		––––––––––––––––––––––––

You must adapt the system which suits your material best.

If Speaker B is very keen to get a turn, he/she might be anticipating where Speaker A is going to finish a turn. In this case, Speaker B starts a turn so quickly that there is not even time for a micropause. If there is neither a pause nor any overlapping of speech, this is known as latching on. It is indicated by equals signs at the end of the first speaker's turn and at the beginning of the second speaker's turn as follows:

Diagram of latching on

Tape no.	Line no.	Speaker	
001	1	A	-------------------------
	2		--------- =
	3	B	= -----------
	4		---------------------

Here the speaker latches on at the end of Speaker A's turn half-way through line 2.

A final possibility is that Speaker B might interrupt Speaker A before he/she is finished. The overlapping speech runs parallel and is usually bracketed together in some way. Sometimes just the beginning of the overlapping speech is bracketed together, but it is useful if both the beginning and the end of the overlap are marked, so that the extent of simultaneous speech is clear. The overlapping speech in the following diagram is marked by double slanted lines ∥ at the beginning and end. However, { } or [ ] could be used instead.

Diagram of simultaneous or overlapping speech

Tape no.	Line no.	Speaker	
001	1	A	-----------------------
	2		----- ∥ -------- ∥
	3	B	(.h)∥---------∥ ---
	4		---------------------

Here Speaker A continues speaking two-thirds of the way

along line 2 but Speaker B starts when Speaker A is only one-third of the way along. The central portion of lines 2 and 3 represents the place where Speakers A and B overlap – they are speaking at the same time. Of course, this makes it very difficult to hear what either one is saying, and this becomes even more difficult if more speakers are involved.

The following two extracts from conversations from a project on a radio phone-in programme show a typical conversation layout:

Transcription of a radio phone-in conversation (CR3)

Key
AR – Alan Robson, the host
I   – Ian, the first caller
A   – Andrea, the second caller
(.)   – micropause
(1.0) – timed pause
(.h) – pause + in-breath
∥. . .∥ – overlapping
=   – latch-on

Tape no.	Line no.	Speaker	
015	1	AR	hello Ian (.)
	2	I	hello (.)
	3	AR	hello (.)
	4	I	(.h)em (.)
	5		I'm just (.) I'm at work at the minute like
	6		so I just phoned up so I could get on and
	7		(.) ∥ so th. ∥ (.) the lads could hear us (.)
	8	AR	∥ right ∥
	9		okay [laughs] what do you want to talk
	10	I	about =
	11		= em (.) well just coming back to
	12		what you mentioned earlier on about
	13		beauty contests an' whether they should
020	14		be (.) or not˙. . .

....

```
022   15   AR   hello Andrea (.)
      16   A                     hello (.)
      17   AR                         hello (1.0)
      18   A                                    hello
      19         Alan (.)
      20   AR              hello (.)
      21   A                        I'm very nervous I'm a
      22         first time caller (.)
      23   AR                         right (.) what would you
      24         like to talk about (.)
025   25   A                             em acid music (.)
```

A brief survey while you're transcribing might reveal quite a bit about the turn-taking in your material. In the extracts here, generally speaking, the turn-taking is quite orderly for a conversation. There is only one short piece of overlapping (lines 7–8). This is presumably because too much overlapping on a radio programme would make the speech unintelligible as the speakers cannot see each other and have no visual cues to help them understand what is going on. A successful host has to judge from the pauses when to begin a turn without causing chaos.

Most of the pauses in these extracts are micropauses. Again, this can be attributed to the nature of the medium. Long silences can cause listeners to think that the programme has finished, or that the station has gone off the air, or that the radio has broken down. This makes the longer pause in line 17 rather awkward. The host must have wondered if he had lost contact with the caller. If the pause had gone on much longer, he would probably have been forced to abandon the call and begin another one.

The two calls can be contrasted in that the first caller is more confident. Only three turns are needed before this caller gets into his stride. Moreover, he is so keen that he latches on in line 11 when the host asks what he wants to talk about.

In contrast, the second caller is more nervous. We can tell this both from the turn-taking and what she says. It takes five turns with a longer pause in the middle before she gets going.

She also waits for the host to pause before she announces her topic.

In summary, the transcription has allowed us to make comments about the medium, the skill of the host and the attitudes of the callers. It illustrates how important an accurate transcription of overlapping, micropauses, in-breaths, hesitations, repetitions and such like is.

Exercise 2

If your spoken material involves more than one speaker, transcribe it using the conventions suggested, making sure that your transcription is accurate. Make a note of any interesting language features that occur to you as you transcribe, so that you can examine these later.

7.3 Prosodic transcription

Prosodic or suprasegmental features of speech are those which occur over and above the individual sounds or segments. They include features such as volume, speed, pitch or tone, rhythm or stress, and other paralinguistic features of voice quality such as whispering or laughing. Obviously, there are certain types of project where such features might be important. For instance, if you are studying a sports commentary of a football match, it may be important to note where the commentator conveys the excitement of an approaching goal by increasing in speed and volume, or where he/she avoids embarrassing pauses or hesitations by holding on to a syllable of a word while he/she thinks of what to say next or until he/she decides what has happened on the pitch.

If you are trying to characterise the idiolect (the individual speech) of a speaker, then you may need to mark prosodic features which indicate the voice quality. Specifying what identifies an individual's voice as unique is not an easy thing to do, although one or two general comments can usually be made. For example, Patrick Moore, the well-known astronomer, is renowned for the speed at which he talks, having received several awards for this phenomenon. Voice quality might also be important in radio or television advertisements.

If you are studying the way in which a mother talks to a young child, then it might be necessary to show exaggerated intonation patterns. Some accents have different stress patterns from RP. If your project involves such an accent, you may need to mark stress on your transcription.

However, if the variety of English that you are studying does not have any significant prosodic features, then there is no need to mark any prosodic features on your transcription. There is not a great deal of point in doing a painstaking analysis of the intonation of your transcription if there is nothing more significant than falling tones towards the end of statements or rising tones in some questions, as these are to be expected in many varieties of English and it is probably not worth drawing attention to this in your analysis.

7.3.1 General trends

Some prosodic features involving volume, speed, pitch and such like can be marked in the margin alongside your transcription. A list of prosodic terms which might be useful for your project are listed below. They have been adapted from Crystal and Davy (1969) *Investigating English Style*. Linguists sometimes use Italian terms from music as these are often more convenient. They are given in the lists alongside their English equivalents. Since the terms are written in the margin of a transcription, they are often abbreviated – that is why some of the endings occur in round brackets in the lists. For example, if you wanted to be learned and use *fortissimo* instead of *very loud* or *v. loud*, you could abbreviate it to *fortiss* or *ff*. You may not need to use many of the terms from the following lists, but they are set out for reference purposes.

Volume/loudness

loud	– f(orte)
very loud	– fortiss(imo) or ff
soft/quiet	– p(iano)

very quiet   – pianiss(imo) or pp
increasing volume to loud – cresc(endo)
decreasing volume   – dim(inuendo)

You could add other musical terms if necessary; for example,
moderately soft: mp; moderately loud: mf.

Speed/pace
fast   – alleg(ro)
very fast   – allegriss(imo)
slow   – lent(o)
very slow   – lentiss(imo)
increasing speed – accel(erando)
decreasing speed – rall(entando)

Pitch range
h(igh)   – talking with a higher pitch than normal
l(ow)   – talking with a lower pitch than normal
monot(one) – not varying the pitch much at all
n(arrow)   – less difference between high and low than
                  normal; for example, a statement might fall less
                  than normal and a question might rise less than
                  normal
w(ide)   – greater difference between high and low than
                  normal; for example, a statement might fall
                  more than normal and a question might rise
                  more than normal
ascend(ing) – going up in pitch
descend(ing) – going down in pitch

An alternative way of marking a sudden step up or step down in
pitch on a particular word would be to use arrows before the
word involved rather than putting abbreviations in the margin:

↑ – a step-up in pitch
↓ – a step-down in pitch

Rhythm
rhythmic – if the speech has a regular beat
arhythmic – distorted or very irregular rhythm

It may also be necessary to indicate the stresses or beats on the actual transcription with these two terms.

stac(cato) – jerky and clipped
gliss(ando) – gliding, smooth and sliding
legato   – drawled
spiky   – sharp

The above terms are marked in the margin, but some symbols can be used on individual sounds or syllables:

clipped sounds or syllable – lȯt
drawled sounds or syllable – a̳nd
held sounds or syllable   – b̲u̲t̲

Tension
This is to do with how tense the muscles of the throat are. They may be:

tense   – if you listen to tapes of RP speakers of 50 years ago, you will notice that their speech seems more tense than the speech of RP speakers today
lax   – the opposite of tense – the muscles are relaxed or loose
precise – great care is taken over every sound or syllable, so that little assimilation (making adjacent sounds similar) or elision (omission of sounds) occurs; both assimilation and elision (for example, *hambag* for *handbag*) are common in normal continuous speech; precise speech is the sort you might use in a formal interview or a prepared speech situation
slurred – often associated with drunks

Other paralinguistic features

Paralinguistic is used here for other sound features rather than for body language. Another term which could be used is voice quality. Most of the terms are self-evident, but some examples of well-known characters who speak in this way are suggested to help you:

whisper	
breathy	– (Sir Robin Day)
husky	– (David Essex)
creak	– brought about by slow vocal cord vibration until the voice creaks (Roger Moore)
fals(etto)	– exceptionally high voice as used by a man imitating a woman (Dame Edna Everidge, yodelling)
reson(ant)	– voice resounds as if mouth is cavernous (opera singing)
spread	– lips spread as a ventriloquist might do
laugh	
giggle	
trem(ulousness)	– shakiness
cry	
sob	

As before, you may need to invent terms of your own if something occurs in your project which is not described in these lists.

Before examining stress and tone in more detail, it's a good idea to have a look at some typical extracts. The following are from a project about football commentary. The transcription makes use of some of the general prosodic features already discussed and it shows how quotation marks can be used to identify the piece of transcription affected. Quotation marks around a piece of transcription mean that the piece of speech is said in the way indicated by the prosodic word enclosed in quotation marks in the margin.

General prosodic transcription of football commentary (CR4)

Key

(.)	– micropause
(.h)	– pause + in-breath
(2.0)	– timed pause
" " *and* ' '	– quotation marks in the transcription correspond to the relevant prosodic features with quotation marks in the margin
cresc	– crescendo, increasing volume
ascend	– ascending pitch
accel	– accelerando, increasing speed
rall	– rallentando, slowing down
dim	– diminuendo, decreasing volume
descend	– descending pitch
laugh	– speaker laughs
a̲n̲d	– held sound(s)
.	– unfinished word

Tape no.	Line no.	Speaker	Prosodics	
027	1	A		Hogg's over to
	2			cover (.h) headed
	3			back in there by
	4			Pointon inside the
	5		"cresc &	penalty are. (.h)
	6		ascend"	" 'Clarke is there
030	7		'accel'	Walsh is there' (.)
	8		'rall'	'Clarke must
	9			score (.)' "
	10		"dim &	"Clarke has
	11		descend"	scored has he
	12			(2.0) and what is
	13			the referee's
	14			decision"

031	15	B		two one the score
	16			line (1.0) <u><u>and</u></u>
033	17			(3.0) [tann<u>oy</u>]
	18			John Macphail's
	19			third of the <u><u></u></u>
	20			season . . .

....

034	21	B		Mel. Kelvin
	22			Morton (1.0) gets
	23			er (1.0) a lot of (.)
036	24		"laugh"	abuse from "the
	25			Brighton fans"
	26			but er those
	27			Sunderland
	28			supporters away
	29			on the far side
	30			aren't
	31			complaining . . .

In the first extract, the commentator speeds up his voice (accel) and becomes louder (cresc) and higher (ascend) as a goal is scored. Afterwards, he slows down (rall) and his voice becomes quieter (dim) and lower (descend). This variation keeps the audience interested. In the second extract, the commentator holds on to the initial sounds of *and* and the final sounds of *Macphail's* while he thinks of something to say about Macphail's action. By doing this, he has avoided an embarrassing pause. In the third extract, the commentator conveys his amusement as he laughs quietly while actually speaking.

If there are lots of prosodic features, and if these features overlap, it is not always easy to indicate them clearly with quotation marks. For example, Speaker A in the football commentary starts to slow down (rall) before reaching his highest (ascend) and loudest (cresc) voice. The way this has been dealt with here is to use the same system as for speech within speech, with sets of double quotation marks on the outside to indicate getting louder and higher (cresc & ascend), and sets of single quotation marks on the inside to indicate firstly speeding up (accel) and then slowing down (rall):

accel (getting faster)   rall (getting slower)

" 'Clarke is there Walsh is there (.)'   'Clarke must score (.)' "

cresc (getting louder) & ascend (getting higher)

The single and double quotation mark system had to be used here because the book is printed in black and white. A better way of solving the problem in your own transcription might be to use various colours (green, black, blue, red and so on) for the various sets of quotation marks or for the words them-selves. Another possibility is to underline the words in different colours. Whichever system you use, you must note it in your key. You should work out a system which will suit your own particular project.

Exercise 3

If any general prosodic features are important to the spoken variety that you have chosen to study for your project, add these to your transcription. If you add any prosodic features, then you should discuss them in your analysis, otherwise there is no point in transcribing them. Conversely, if you discuss prosodic features in your analysis, then you should really mark them in your transcription. If there is nothing interesting to say about volume, speed, pitch range or voice quality, and it is not part of your aim to look at these, then do not add anything to your basic transcription.

7.3.2   Stress
As stress and tone cause a great deal of confusion among students, we will look at them in some detail. If stress and tone are not particularly relevant to your project, then it is a good idea to skim read this material, as it becomes increasingly

difficult as we proceed. Many of the examples used here are from Pellowe (1976).

The confusion between stress and tone occurs partly because a syllable with a prominent change in direction of tone is also likely to be strongly stressed. However, a stressed syllable often has no prominent change in tone, so you should not be marking every stressed syllable that you hear with tones.

The confusion between stress and tone also occurs because there are various ways of indicating them. You may, for instance, already be familiar with methods of marking metre in poetry. Frequently, the symbols ‾ and ˘ are used above syllables. This is different from the way that stress is marked in ordinary language use by linguists.

It is usual to think of each syllable as being either stressed or unstressed (that is, weakly stressed). Syllables which are usually unstressed include the 'small' grammatical or function words such as prepositions (for example, *to*), conjunctions (for example, *and*), articles (for example, *a/an* and *the*), auxiliary verbs (for example, forms of HAVE and BE) and some pro-forms (for example, *I* and *he*). Unstressed syllables are left unmarked by linguists. Because they are unstressed, they are often reduced in form (for example, *'n'* for *and*). A useful tip for identifying function words is to look for the words which would be left out in a telegram.

The items which carry stress on one of their syllables are the main nouns and verbs of an utterance. Linguists mark stress on these syllables by using a ' before the stressed syllable. Thus, a normal rendering of *They've eaten the chickens* would involve a stress on the first syllable of the main verb *eaten* and a stress on the first syllable of the main noun *chickens* as follows:

They've 'eaten the 'chickens

There is little stress on the pronoun *They*, the auxiliary verb *'ve*, the definite article *the*, or the second syllables of *eaten* and *chickens*. Notice that stress is the property of the syllable, not of the whole word, unless of course the word consists of only one syllable. Many basic words in English have stress on their first syllable, but polysyllabic words can vary:

    'telegraph   te'legraphy   tele'graphic

There is little point in marking stress in a transcription if it is normal, as in the renderings of *They've 'eaten the 'chickens*, *'telegraph*, *te'legraphy* and *tele'graphic*. There would be little of interest to say in your analysis and you could spend a very long time doing the transcription. However, if part of your aim is to look at normal English stress patterns, then a small section marked for stress would probably suffice.

A more practical and interesting approach is to mark stress only where it is significantly different from the normal stress pattern. Thus, it might be significant if a syllable which is normally unstressed carries stress, or if a syllable which is normally stressed carries extra strong stress. A way of marking this extra strong stress is by using " before the syllable. This indicates contrastive stress:

    "I can't help you every day
    He "tells me his father's a millionaire

I is normally unstressed. Stressing it heavily implies that someone else can help but not the speaker. *Tell* is normally stressed. Giving it extra strong stress implies that the speaker doesn't necessarily believe him.

Other reasons for marking stress in a transcription might be if the speech is very rhythmical or if the speaker of an accent under consideration is using different stress patterns from an RP speaker. For instance, natives of the North-East of England are likely to say:

    New'castle

while RP speakers usually say:

    'Newcastle

Here are some extracts from a transcription in which stress is unusual:

Transcriptions involving stress (CR5)

' – placed before a syllable to indicate stress; used on unusual
  items only
" – placed before a strongly stressed syllable

Tape no.	Line no.	Speaker	
039	1	DC	John gave a book to Fred and
	2		"he gave one to Mary

....

041	3	AC	nineteen thirty nine when war
	4		broke out I seed the
	5		adver'tisement in the
	6		newspaper

In the first extract, the strong stress on *he* tells us that it was Fred who gave the book to Mary. The marking of strong stress is vital to the interpretation of the sentence. If no stress had been marked, the sentence would have been taken to mean that it was John who had given the book to Mary.

The second extract is adapted from the book *Varieties of English* by Freeborn with Langford and French (1986). In it, the speaker, Mrs Amy Cook, from Wotton-under-Edge in Gloucestershire, stresses the third syllable rather than the second in the word *adver'tisement*. An RP speaker would say *ad'vertisement*. The alteration in stress by Amy Cook means that the vowel sound in *tise* changes. It becomes a stressed /aɪ/ rather than an unstressed /ɪ/ or /ə/.

The placement of stress on polysyllabic words has been the subject of much controversy (*con'troversy* or *'controversy?*). The older pattern, which has been adopted by the BBC, involves stress on the first syllable (*'controversy*). The newer convention has stress on the second syllable (*con'troversy*).

Prescriptivists who dislike change would like to impose the older convention on us all.

The following further dimension can be added to the description of stress in your project, if necessary. Some linguists use a system of notation which involves both primary and secondary stress. They suggest that words of two or more syllables can have a syllable which is not as strongly stressed as the syllable with primary stress but has more stress than weakly stressed syllables. Certain word classes such as adjectives are also seen as having an intermediate kind of stress sometimes. Secondary stress is shown with a stress mark before the syllable concerned but below it rather than above it.

Secondary stress might be useful in distinguishing compound words from phrases:

compound	noun phrase with adjective
'black,bird	,black 'bird

In the compound word *blackbird*, it is the first syllable which has primary stress, while the noun *bird*, which would normally be stressed, has a less prominent secondary stress. In the phrase *black bird*, the main stress is on the noun *bird*, while secondary stress occurs on the adjective *black*.

Secondary stress can also be important when discussing the distinction between word classes. For example, the verb *prophesy* and the noun *prophecy* are distinguished in spelling but the verb can also be differentiated from the noun because the last syllable of the verb has secondary stress:

verb	noun
'prophe,sy	'prophecy

Note that the extra secondary stress on the verb *prophesy* has altered the pronunciation of the last vowel. RP speakers would probably pronounce the last syllable of the verb *prophesy* as /saɪ/, while they would probably pronounce the last syllable of the noun *prophecy* as /sɪ/. This change is similar to the one which occurs when Amy Cook pronounces *adver'tisement* rather than *ad'vertisement*, although the different spellings of

the two words *prophesy* and *prophecy* disguise the correspondence to some extent.

Finally, secondary stress could be useful if you are studying
American English, as American English speakers often place
the primary stress in a different place from British English
speakers, yet they still retain a vestige of stress on another
syllable. Thus, the main stress on the word *military* for a British
English speaker is on the first syllable, while for an American
it is on the third syllable. However, the first syllable still retains
some stress:

British English   *American English*
 'military   ,mili'tary

In summary, when marking stress on transcriptions, concentrate on those syllables which are unusual in some way. They
may be rhythmically stressed or contrastively stressed, or
stressed when they wouldn't normally be. Focus on primary
stress in the first instance and include secondary stress if
necessary.

Exercise 4

If there are any interesting stress patterns in your transcription
which need to be commented on in your project, mark them
using ' and " where necessary.

7.3.3   Tone units, prominent words, tonic syllables and tones
In speech, information is conveyed in tone or information units
rather than in sentences or clauses. If you listen to people
speaking, you should be able to identify a group of words that
hangs together intonationally. The identity of the group can be
spotted by things such as short pauses, abrupt changes in pitch
and volume, or lengthening of the last speech sound in the
group. Each tone or information unit has a prominent word
within it which stands out from the rest. The boundary of the
tone or information unit is marked by | and the most prominent
word in the group is often denoted by bold type. Since bold

type may not be available to you in your project work, the prominent words have been underlined here.

The following extract is from a conversation between two women in their twenties. Try reading it out loud.

A transcription with tone units and prominent words

Key
(.)   – micropause
(1.0)   – timed pause
| – tone unit boundary
underlining – prominent word in the tone unit

Line no.	Speaker	
1	Claire	mm	(.) a friend of <u>mine</u> who is a	(1.0)
2		<u>well</u>	at the <u>moment</u>	he's a <u>supply</u>
3		teacher	what <u>happened</u>	he he was
4		working at a school in <u>Fulham</u>	(.) and
5		then he went to <u>America</u>	(.) for (.) the
6		summer <u>well</u>	for three <u>months</u>	<u>actually</u>
7			(.) and so he didn't get <u>back</u>	till the end
8		of <u>October</u>	

The most likely time when you might need to mark tone units is if the units are unusually long or short, and this is a significant feature in your project. For example, the following long tone unit contains several clauses and is spoken in a hurried and breathless manner:

can't stop I went to Julie's and we went swimming and now I'm late <u>home</u> |

In contrast, this old cricket commentary has the information packaged in small units which are easily digested by the audience:

thirty <u>four</u> for | <u>two</u> | (.) <u>Edrich</u> | (.) twenty <u>two</u> | (.) and <u>Cowdrey</u> | <u>out</u> | this <u>morning</u> |

Marking prominent words shows which bits of the information are considered most important by the speaker. The following two extracts from radio advertisements have small, easy-to-process tone units, show emphasis on the words which the companies believe to be important in the marketing of their products, and occasionally display marked usage in the placement of a prominent word in a tone unit.

Transcription of radio advertisements showing tone units and prominent words (CR6)

Key
(.)   – micropause
(1.0) – timed pause
| – tone unit boundary
_____ – prominent word in the tone unit

Tape no.	Line no.	Speaker	
045	1	male RP	if you're buying a <u>car</u> | (.) <u>we</u>
	2		set the <u>pace</u> | (.) this is the
	3		<u>name</u> | (.) <u>Patterson's</u> | (2.0)
	4		this is the <u>place</u> |

....

	5		are your <u>teeth</u> sensitive | and
	6		sometimes react <u>painfully</u> |
	7		(1.0) do hot and cold <u>drinks</u> |
	8		make you <u>worse</u> | if they
	9		touch your <u>teeth</u> | (2.0) <u>try</u> |
052	10		<u>new</u> | <u>Dentrex</u> | <u>toothpaste</u> |

In some cases in these radio advertisements, it is not always easy to distinguish the most prominent word in the group, or indeed the group of words that hang together, since many of the lexical words carry quite a lot of stress. An example of this is *re'act* in line 6. Going by the pauses sometimes helps. However, it is difficult to decide, for instance, how many tone units there are between *do* and *teeth* in lines 7 to 9. The prominent words seem to be connected with the product (*car*, *toothpaste*), the name of the company or the brand name (*Patterson's*, *Dentrex*) and any words associated with these (*name*, *place*; *teeth*, *painfully*, *drinks*, *worse*, *new* and the imperative *try* which urges the listener to act).

A marked use of a prominent word occurs in line 1 where *we* is at the beginning of the tone unit. The stress on this first person pronoun emphasises the personal nature of the company and stresses Patterson's as opposed to other dealers. Similarly, in lines 9 and 10, marked usage of four tone units instead of one highlights the product name, with prominence being given to the pre-modifier *Dentrex* which under normal circumstances would not be exceptionally prominent.

Once you have identified the tone unit and the most prominent word in it, you should be able to identify the tonic syllable. The tonic syllable is the stressed syllable of the prominent word. It is called the tonic syllable because there is some change of direction of tone on it. For example, the tonic syllable is the first syllable in *Dentrex*. The tonic syllable can be shown by putting it in capital letters: *DENtrex*.

The greatest difficulty is in identifying which way the tone is going: down (falling), up (rising) or a combination of both (fall-rise or rise-fall). This is not made any easier by the fact that your voice often has to fall slightly before it can rise and vice versa. Thus, ordinary falling and rising tones can sometimes be mistaken for more complex rise-falls and fall-rises. The picture is further complicated because of regional differences in intonation. Even experts have trouble sometimes in agreeing on their perceptions on the direction of tones, and machines apparently are not a great deal of help in the analysis because they often fail to pick out, from among the detail, the features which are important to the interpretation given by speakers and hearers.

Spotting the direction of tones takes a good deal of practice. The following rules of thumb for identifying tones might be helpful:

1   A **falling tone** ˋ expresses certainty, completeness and independence. It has an air of finality. A straightforward statement normally ends with a falling tone:

   it's five o'CLÒCK | (.) here is the NÈWS |

2   A **rising tone** ´ expresses uncertainty, incompleteness and dependence. A yes–no question (but not a *wh*-question) usually has a rising tone; as do dependent clauses or afterthoughts, and lists before the final item which ends in a falling tone:

   are you LÉAving |
   if you LÍKE | we can go for a PÌCnic |
   BÚtter | ÉGGS | SÚgar | and about 250 grams of FLOÙR |

   Polite commands or denials may have rising tones; otherwise they sound rude:

   A: are you BÚsy |
   B: ŃO |
        do sit DÓWN |

3   A **level tone** ˉ is rarer but may express boredom or sarcasm:

   shall I do it NŌW |

4   A **fall-rise** ˇ combines assertion and certainty with dependence and incompleteness, so usually suggests reservation:

   A: do you like PÓP music |
   B: SǑMEtimes | (but not in general)
   A: are you BÚsy |
   B: not RĚAlly | (well I am but you can interrupt if you want)

5 A **rise-fall** ^ may express pleasure:

we have the LÂRgest | country house in the WÔRLD |

As can be seen, marking the tonic syllable is difficult, not only because it is sometimes hard to say in which direction the tone is going, but because with words of two syllables or more it is not always easy to know where to put the syllable division. Sometimes several answers are equally acceptable.

As with other prosodic features, it is really only necessary to mark tones if they strike you as being unusual or important to the interpretation. You may spot an attitude of enthusiasm, sympathy, encouragement, surprise, scolding, urgency, frustration and so on. You may then be able to link this with a particular change in tone. Even if you can't tell the direction of the tone movement, you should have little difficulty in spotting the attitude conveyed.

If the tones in your spoken material show a fall on the last stressed syllable of declaratives functioning as statements, or a rise on the last stressed syllable of interrogatives functioning as questions, then there is not much point in doing a painstaking analysis of the tones. If the tones in some parts of your spoken material are unusual, it may be worth spending some time in selectively marking them.

The following two extracts show interesting uses of tones:

Transcriptions with tones (CR7)

Key
´	– rising tone	
ˇ	– fall-rise tone	selectively
JOB	– tonic syllable in capital letters	marked
|	– tone unit boundary	

Tape no.	Line no.	Speaker	
055	1	DC	Fred's got a new JÓB |

....

056   2   A   will you come out tonight (.)
           3   B   YĚS |

In the first extract, you would expect a falling tone on the declarative *Fred's got a new job*. The rising tone on JÓB indicates this is questioning or surprising. If the tone hadn't been marked, the sentence would have been interpreted as an ordinary statement.

In the second extract, the fall-rise on YĚS by Speaker B suggests reticence and to some extent contradicts the meaning conveyed by *yes*. It is necessary to mark the tone in order to convey the exact nuance of the reply.

Some linguists add further sophistication to the five tone types already listed. They make a distinction within rising and falling between high and low: high rising ´, low rising ˌ, high falling ˋ, low falling ˎ. This allows you to distinguish, for instance, between extreme disbelief and a calmer, quieter kind of urgency:

high rising: let's have a cup of TÉA |
                  (How on earth can you think of tea in such a crisis)
low rising: please don't WOrry |
                  (I urge you not to worry)

and between a factual, straightforward statement and an exclamation involving mild surprise and liveliness:

low falling: let's have a cup of TEA |
                  (unmarked usage)
high falling: I think she's deLÌGHTful |
                  (lively usage)

There are other ways of indicating both stress and tone in speech. One way involves a kind of musical notation in which every syllable is represented by a dot. Large dots show the stressed syllables while a tail on a dot, rather like a tadpole, shows the tonic syllable. The way the tail points indicates whether the tone is rising or falling. The following three examples show how saying *Let's have a cup of tea* in three different ways with different tones on *tea* would look with this kind of musical notation:

1

Let's have a cup of tea

●　　·　　·　●　　·　◣

Unmarked usage with a straightforward interpretation.

2

Let's have a cup of tea

●　　·　　·　●　　·　◞

High rising expressing extreme surprise; for example, 'How on earth can you think of tea in such a crisis'.

3

Let's have a cup of tea

●　　·　　·　●　　·　◝

Rise-fall expressing pleasure; for example, 'Now that we're back in a country where we can get it'.

One advantage of this system is that it gives you a readily identifiable profile of the whole utterance. You can see that the stressed syllables are *let's*, *cup* and *tea*; that the unstressed syllables are *have*, *a* and *of*; and that the tonic syllables in all of these are on the word *tea*.

If you wanted a simpler system to show the overall intonation of the sentence without showing the stressed, unstressed and tonic syllables, you could adapt this system using merely dashes or a continuous line to show the pitch height:

4

Let's have a cup of tea

‾ ‾ ‾ ‾ ‾ ＼

Unmarked usage with a straightforward interpretation.

5

Let's have a cup of tea

Ｖ

High rising expressing extreme surprise.

If we move the tonic syllable to an unusual position in *Let's have a cup of tea* (that is, not near the end of the sentence), we can obtain further interpretations:

6

Let's have a cup of tea

⌐　· ·　●　·　●

Tonic syllable on *let's* suggests an interpretation of: 'There's no harm in changing your mind'.

7

Let's have a cup of tea

●　·　·　⌐　·　●

Tonic syllable on *cup* suggests an interpretation of: 'We won't have a pot today'.

The musical notation allows us to show that after the fall on *let's* or *cup* the rest of the utterance continues at a low level. However, if you do not need to show this, then examples 6 and 7 could be transcribed more simply by using contrastive stress " on *"let's* and *"cup*, in which case you would not need to make decisions about the directions of the tones.

In summary, one of the main problems of marking tones in transcriptions is that students tend to regard them like stresses and sprinkle them going in all directions, even on unstressed syllables and whole words rather than just on the tonic syllable. An important point to remember if you are going to transcribe tones is that only one syllable in the group is marked for tone. Normally, this is the last stressed syllable in the tone unit. If the tones are placed in unusual positions or are of an unusual type, you will probably notice these as striking. If not, your spoken material may not be worth transcribing with tones. If you have problems in deciding the tone types, or in syllable division for tonic syllables, then you may be able to concentrate only on the tone or information units, or the prominent words, or on giving an overall intonation profile of the utterance using dashes or a continuous line.

Exercise 5

Mark the tone units and prominent words, or the tonic syllables and tones, on your transcription where these are unusual or interesting. You may want to confine yourself to tone units and prominent words if you have difficulty in deciding which way the tones are going. If there is nothing interesting to say about any of these features, do not mark them on your transcription.

7.4   Phonetic transcription

This section deals with phonetic transcription in some detail, as, like the prosodic features discussed in the previous section, this is a new area of spoken English for many students. If you are unlikely to need phonetic symbols in your transcription, you could skim read this section and proceed to Chapter 8, where the next stage in tackling a project is explained.

If you are going to discuss pronunciation at all in your project, then you will definitely need to use the phonetic alphabet. It is no good relying on an attempt to represent pronunciation in normal spelling, as the letters of the alphabet can be used for a variety of sounds.

The phonetic symbols you use should be based on the International Phonetic Alphabet (IPA) which is the most widely accepted system. It is also the system which is used to represent pronunciation in modern dictionaries for both foreign languages and English. However, you need to be aware that there are simplified and typewritten versions of phonetic alphabets, but you must try not to let these confuse you. You also need to know that linguists may use slightly different IPA symbols for the same sound if the sound in question falls somewhere between what the two symbols represent. An example of this is the use of both /ɛ/ and /e/ for the RP sound in the middle of *bed*.

RP, Received Pronunciation, is so called because it was the accent which was accepted or received at court and in the higher classes of society. It is the sort of accent which national news-readers use. RP is the accent which has been studied the most and against which all other accents are contrasted, although it has been estimated that it is spoken by only 3 to 5 per cent of the population of Britain. This means that if you are studying an accent, you need to be able to judge what the RP pronunciation of a word is likely to be. This is not always easy as RP speakers themselves vary.

One of the most widely used set of phonetic symbols is that occurring in Gimson's (1980) *An Introduction to the Pronunciation of English*. The book is useful as a reference book as it contains a list of the symbols for RP, as well as other IPA symbols which can be used for local accents, if necessary. Each section about an RP sound also includes variants used in other parts of the country. If you cannot decide which symbol to use for a local sound you are transcribing, you may spot a useful symbol in the relevant section of Gimson's book.

Gimson divides the vowels into long and short, although not all linguists do this. The long vowels are indicated by two dots after them. In project work, this may be useful because absence of length often allows a distinction to be made between older and modern versions of RP. The older version is often more clipped. Length marks are also useful for distinguishing between sounds in some local accents. For instance, in the North, /e/ can be used for the sound in the middle of *bed* while /e:/ can be used for the vowel in *pay*. The long vowels are the ones which tend to be equivalent to diphthongs (two vowels running into one sound) in other accents. For example, Northern /e:/ in *pay* is equivalent to the diphthong /eɪ/ in RP.

The slanting lines around the sounds distinguish them from letters. They really indicate that the sounds in question are phonemes operating in a sound system in a particular accent. Detailed phonetic differences are usually shown in brackets [   ]. However, the distinction between phonology, the study of sounds or phonemes in a system, and phonetics, the detailed study of sounds without regard to their appearance in a system, is difficult to grasp at this level. Thus, all sounds discussed here are shown in slanting lines, even though they may sometimes represent detailed phonetic differences in accents.

An adapted version of Gimson's RP phonemes is listed below. These sounds can be heard on the cassette tape accompanying Freeborn's (1986) *Varieties of English*.

Vowels

1   Simple vowels (monophthongs)
     (a)   Five long vowels
            /i:/   bead   /bi:d/
            /ɑ:/   bard   /bɑ:d/
            /ɔ:/   board   /bɔ:d/
            /u:/   shoe   /ʃu:/
            /ɜ:/   bird   /bɜ:d/
     (b)   Seven short vowels
            /ɪ/   bid   /bɪd/
            /e/   bed   /bed/   (some linguists use /ɛ/ here)
            /æ/   bad   /bæd/
            /ɒ/   cod   /kɒd/
            /ʊ/   put   /pʊt/   (some linguists use /ɷ/ here)
            /ʌ/   cup   /kʌp/
            /ə/   the   /ðə/   (this symbol is called a
                       about   /əbaʊt/   schwa /ʃwɑ:/ and occurs
                       porter   /pɔ:tə/   in most unstressed syl-
                                             lables)

2 Diphthongs

   (a)   Three diphthongs end in /ɪ/ where the tongue moves to the front of the mouth:

/eɪ/	pay	/peɪ/
/aɪ/	pie	/paɪ/
/ɔɪ/	boy	/bɔɪ/

   (b)   Two diphthongs end in /ʊ/ where the tongue moves to the back of the mouth:

/əʊ/	go	/gəʊ/
/aʊ/	hound	/haʊnd/ (conservative or marked RP speakers may use /ɑʊ/)

   (c)   Three diphthongs end in /ə/ where the tongue moves to the middle of the mouth:

/ɪə/	beer	/bɪə/
/ɛə/	bear	/bɛə/
/ʊə/	cure	/kjʊə/

Consonants

/p/	pit	/pɪt/
/b/	bit	/bɪt/
/t/	tip	/tɪp/
/d/	did	/dɪd/
/k/	kick	/kɪk/
/g/	give	/gɪv/
/f/	five	/faɪv/
/v/	vine	/vaɪn/
/θ/	thumb	/θʌm/
/ð/	this	/ðɪs/
/s/	some	/sʌm/
/z/	zoo	/zu:/
/ʃ/	shoe	/ʃu:/
/ʒ/	measure	/meʒə/
/h/	hot	/hɒt/
/tʃ/	charge	/tʃɑ:dʒ/
/dʒ/	gin	/dʒɪn/
/m/	mouse	/maʊs/
/n/	nice	/naɪs/
/ŋ/	sing	/sɪŋ/
/l/	leaf	/li:f/

/r/	run	/rʌn/
/j/	yacht	/jɒt/
/w/	wet	/wet/

Many of the RP symbols can be used when transcribing other accents, even if the sounds occur in different places than they do in RP. For example, Northern varieties of English do not have /ʌ/ in *cup* but a sound more like /ʊ/ or even /ə/. Cockney *pay* does not have the RP vowel /eɪ/ but is more like the RP sound /aɪ/ in *pie*. If you want to be more precise, you could make up symbols of your own, using the RP ones already provided. For instance, the vowel in cockney *nine* is not /aɪ/. It is a bit like /ɔɪ/ but is really more like /ɑɪ/. The vowel in cockney *down* sounds a bit like what is represented by the more complicated symbol /æə/.

If you have to make up your own symbols, it is helpful if you know which sounds are near each other in the vowel chart. A vowel chart represents a side view of the mouth showing the position of the tongue (and mouth) when pronouncing vowels. The mouth is divided longitudinally into front, centre and back. You need to decide whether the front, centre or back of the tongue is being used. Horizontally, the mouth is divided into four. The tongue can be close to the roof of the mouth or open near the bottom of the mouth. There are two intermediate positions: half-close and half-open. Some of the vowels at the main intersection points on the vowel chart do not occur in RP. These have been marked with an asterisk. However, they may occur in regional accents. /ɛ/ does not occur on its own in RP, only as /ɛə/. A few other RP vowels have also been added to the vowel chart to show where they are in relation to the primary vowels. The vowel chart in Figure 1 might prove a useful reference for you.

If you need help in deciding which symbols to use, Hughes and Trudgill (1979) *English Accents and Dialects* is useful, as it contains a brief survey of various accents in Britain. Trudgill and Hannah (1985) *International English* has information about accents and dialects outside of Britain. Take care, however, as some of the phonetic symbols in both books are different from those used here. In addition, don't assume that an informant in

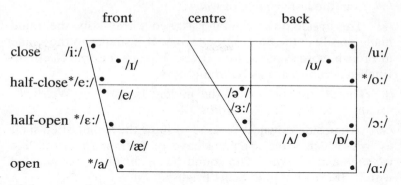

Figure 1 *Vowel chart*

your project, even if from the same region as the informants in the books, will have exactly the same sounds.

One or two symbols not in the list for RP might be useful for transcribing local accents:

/e:/ A monophthong (simple vowel) often used in Northern varieties instead of the RP diphthong /eɪ/ in words such as *pay* (RP /peɪ/, Northern /pe:/). /e:/ is an older sound less affected by the Great Vowel Shift which began earlier in Southern varieties of English where it has been estimated that vowels began to alter from the fourteenth or fifteenth centuries onwards. /e:/ is similar to the vowel used in French *thé* for *tea*.

/o:/ Like /e:/, /o:/ is a Northern monophthong used instead of RP /əʊ/ in words such as *go* (RP /gəʊ/, Northern /go:/). /o:/ has a history similar to /e:/. It is like the sound in French *eau* for *water*.

/ɹ/ This 'r' symbol can be used for the RP sound if a contrast is needed with an accent with a rolled sound, when the ordinary /r/ can be used. The rolled sound, where the tongue repeatedly hits the roof of the mouth, occurs in Scots and Italian varieties. With the RP sound, the tongue remains still behind the tooth ridge.

/ɻ/ A sound with a curl on it indicates that the tongue is curled back more (retroflex), as for 'r' in some South Western varieties of English. Americans also tend to do this with schwas /ɚ/, as in the last syllable of *water*.

/ʁ/   This upside-down capital 'r' is used to transcribe the sound made noisily in the back of the throat. It is similar to the sound in French words such as *très*. It also appears in some Northern English accents such as Northumbrian.

/ɬ/   This 'l' with a curl in the middle is used for Welsh 'l', usually spelt *ll* as in *Llandudno*.

/ʍ/   An upside-down 'w' is used to show the sound often spelt as 'wh' which some speakers have to distinguish words like *whether* and *weather*. The sound has a /h/ quality associated with it. It is common in Scots English.

/x/   This shows the sound made in the back of the throat which Scots use at the end of the word *loch*. Liverpudlians also often use this sound for RP /k/ in words such as *back*.

/ʔ/   A question mark without a dot underneath represents a glottal stop. It usually occurs instead of RP /t/ in the middle or at the end of words. It is formed by briefly closing and opening the glottis ('lips' in the voice box), so that the air is temporarily and very briefly stopped. It is common in many accents in words such as *button*, *bottle* and *butter*, and is even creeping into RP on the end of words followed by another word beginning with a consonant, as in *quite nice*.

/a/   This symbol can be used for the vowel in *bad* which occurs in Northern and some other accents. The sound is made with the mouth more open than for RP /æ/.

Obviously, you will need a phonetic transcription if your project involves an accent. However, you may also need to use it if you are investigating a topic such as child language acquisition. As young children are often unable to pronounce the adult version of a word, it is interesting to discover which sorts of sounds they are unable to produce, and to see if they have generalised some pronunciation rules of their own. In such cases, it is only necessary to transcribe phonetically those words which cause difficulty. An example of a selective phonetic transcription can be seen in the following extract from a study of the language of a two-year-old. The student has phonetically transcribed the words that the child has been unable to pronounce properly underneath the conventional spelling of the word that the child was aiming at. The discussion in the extract is about Christmas presents.

Selective phonetic transcription of the language of a two-year-old (CR8)

Key
D – Dionne
M – Mother
Dale – Dionne's brother
/ / – encloses phonetic transcription of selected words
[ ] – encloses paralinguistic features such as laughter and unclear speech
= – latch-on
(.) – micropause
(2.0) – timed pause

Tape no.	Line no.	Speaker	
060	1	D	bike (.)
	2	M	bike (.) and what else (4.0) pram =
	3	D	= pram /bam/
	4		[laughter and unclear speech]
	5	M	what else (3.0)
	6	D	baby (.)
	7	M	a baby (2.0) and what else (.)
	8	Dale	a hen (1.0) [laughs]
	9	M	do you like Santie (1.0) tell Susie when
	10		you went to see Santa Claus yesterday (.)
067	11	D	see Santa Claus /di: tantə tɔːz/

Even a cursory glance at this transcription suggests some pronunciation differences in the child's usage which would fit well into the patterns suggested in Ingram (1986) 'Phonological patterns in the speech of young children'. Dionne has reduced consonant clusters at the beginning of *pram* and *Claus*. In these two words, she has also managed to avoid the consonants /r/ and /l/, which are often among the last to be mastered. In addition, Dionne has voiced the /p/ at the beginning of *pram*, making it into a /b/. This initial voicing is typical in child language acquisition.

Certain types of consonants (fricatives) cause problems for young children. They are replaced by plosives, which are also known as stops. This 'stopping' can be seen in the use of /t/ and /d/ at the beginning of *Santa* and *see* respectively.

Finally, Dionne also displays consonant harmony. The /t/ at the beginning of *Santa* has affected the /k/ at the beginning of *Claus* which has also become /t/.

All of these pronunciation features have been noted without any mention being made of grammar (no indefinite articles), vocabulary (*baby* for *dolly*), conversation skills and the mother's role, all of which you might find easier to spot than pronunciation difficulties. There is therefore a vast range of features that could be included in a project, even in a short extract such as this. You should get into the habit of jotting down any ideas you have which could be useful for your analysis as you are transcribing.

The following transcription of the language of a North-East club comedian shows a more ambitious use of phonetics in that all of the words are phonetically transcribed but only for a short section of the spoken material. The student discovered that this short section contained all of the accent features she needed to discuss. Using conventions of her own, she tried to show the words which were pronounced identically in RP and the local accent. She also tried to identify the individual sounds which were different in the local accent by underlining them. Since part of the humour of the extract arises when the comedian attempts to imitate RP, the student also identified sounds where the comedian had tried, sometimes unsuccessfully, to imitate RP.

Detailed phonetic transcription of the language of a NE club comedian (CR9)

Key

A – conventional orthography
B – phonetic transcription inside / /
IPA – symbols mainly as in Gimson (1980)
___ – NE (North-East) sounds not in the equivalent RP words
=== – attempts at RP sounds
( ) – places where NE words are usually pronounced the same as in RP
BT – Bobby Thompson
(.) – micropause
(1.0) – timed pause

Tape no.	Line no.	Speaker		
071	1	BT	A:	well I could see Monty [that is, Montgomery]
			B:	/(wel) a̲ kəd sɪi: mɒnti̲
	2		A:	was on edge 'cause he was counting his
			B:	(wəz ɒn edʒ kɒz i wəz) kaʊʔɪn i̲:z
	3		A:	money without looking at it (laughter 3.0)
			B:	mə̲ni̲ (wɪθaʊt) lə̲kɪn a̲r (ɪt)
	4		A:	so I went over to him I says are you
			B:	sᴏ̲: a̲ (went) aʊə tɪv̲ (əm) a̲ se̲:z a̲r (jə)
	5		A:	a bit short (1.0) he says no Bob I've
			B:	a̲ (bɪt ʃɔ:t) i) se̲:z nᴏ̲: (bɒb) a̲v
	6		A:	got a couple of hours to spend and I
			B:	gɒr̲ (ə) kə̲pl (ə) a̲ʊə̲z (tə spend ən) a̲
	7		A:	don't really know where to go (.) I
			B:	də̲ʊnt ri:li̲ nə̲ʊ we̲ə tu̲ gə̲ʊ a̲
	8		A:	says well I'm going over to the Palace
			B:	(sez wel) a̲m gə̲ʊɪn ə̲ʊvə (tə ðə) pa̲ləs
076	9		A:	would you care to accompany me (2.0)
			B:	wʊ̲d ju̲ ke̲ə tu̲ ək̲ʌmpni̲ mi̲:/

There is plenty to write about here concerning NE pronunciation and how it differs from RP, although it is worth noting that 'dropping the aitch' in some words is not necessarily just a regional accent feature, as it also occurs in unstressed words such as *him* in RP in continuous speech.

A quick survey of the transcription shows the following:

RP	NE	Examples
/ʊ/ & /ʌ/ ⟶	/ə/	could, money
/i:/ ⟶	/ɪi:/	see
/ɪ/ ⟶	/i:/	money, Monty
/aɪ/ ⟶	/a/	I
/æ/ ⟶	/a/	Palace
/t/ ⟶	/ʔ/	counting
	/r/	at, got
/ŋ/ ⟶	/n/	counting, looking
/əʊ/ ⟶	/o:/	so
	/aʊ/	over
/eɪ/ ⟶	/e:/	says

In the analysis, these features would have to be organised, perhaps into vowels and consonants with charts and maps if possible. Then each sound could be explained historically, positionally and so on where necessary.

Part of the humour of the transcription arises when the comedian tries to imitate RP. He succeeds with certain sounds:

/əʊ/	don't, know	(NE /o:/)
/ɛə/	where, care	(NE /ɛ:/)
/ʊ/	would	(NE /ə/)
/i:/	me	(NE /ɪi:/)
/ʌ/	accompany	(NE /ə/)

but he overdoes it in other places by using stressed vowels instead of the schwas which would be used in RP. For example, he uses /u:/ in *you* and *to* (RP /ə/). This phenomenon is known as hypercorrection and occurs when an accent speaker tries to speak 'posh' but uses the sound in the wrong place. What makes it even more funny is that in some words there is a mixture of 'posh' RP and the comedian's own NE accent. For example, RP /əʊ/ and NE /n/ both occur in /gəʊɪn/.

Exercise 6

If you need a phonetic transcription, add this to the conventional spelling in your transcription. Selected words or short extracts may be all that are required. An attempt should be made to incorporate these under your main transcription so that the phonetics can be easily checked for accuracy as the tape is played.

Exercise 7

Check your transcription thoroughly. We are so conditioned to normal spelling that it is very easy to make a mistake. The following checklist may be useful.

Phonetic symbol checklist
1   Check the new symbols. Many of the symbols will be familiar to you, as the phonetic alphabet is based on the Roman alphabet, but the following need special attention:

    (a)   The two long vowels, backward 'c' /ɔ:/ and curly three /ɜ:/. These new symbols often occur in words which are spelt with an 'r' or another consonant, as in *bird* and *saw*. The 'r' and 'w' are not present in RP pronunciation. Also check that you have used length marks on vowels where necessary.

    (b)   Four of the short vowels are also new symbols. Ash /æ/ is based on an Old English letter and represents a sound closer to /e/ than /a/. /a/ can be used for Northern and some other varieties of English. RP speakers sound to Northerners as if they are saying something between *bad* and *bed* for *bad*. This is even more so in old RP recordings.

           Speakers of Scots English may have some problems

with backward 'a' /ɒ/, as they tend to have the same sound in both *cot* and *caught*.

Horseshoe or curly 'u' /ʊ/ and upside-down 'v' /ʌ/ cause particular problems to those who speak a Northern variety of English, as they may have only one sound in both *cup* and *put*. Historically, Southerners also had only one sound /ʊ/, which developed into /ʌ/ in some words. Check /ʊ/ and /ʌ/.

Upside-down 'e', known as schwa, occurs very frequently in RP, as it appears in most unstressed syllables whichever vowel is used in the spelling. Thus, function words such as *a*, *and* and *the* are usually unstressed and have /ə/ as a vowel. Schwa also usually occurs, sometimes more than once, in other words with two or more syllables. For example, the underlined syllables in the following words all have schwas in RP: moth<u>er</u>, Chin<u>a</u> and <u>a</u>gainst. Check that you have transcribed schwas where necessary and not the full vowels associated with the spelling.

(c)   The only new diphthong symbol is the Greek 'e' /ɛ/ in /ɛə/. Check this symbol.

(d)   Eight of the consonants have new symbols. /θ/ is from the Greek 'theta' and /ð/ is an Old English symbol called 'eth'. The main problem with these is in differentiating them, as they are often represented in writing by the same symbol, the two letters 'th'. The difference between the two sounds is that /θ/ is the voiceless sound and /ð/ is voiced. You will feel the difference if you put your fingers over your Adam's apple and say *thumb* and *this* slowly. The first word begins with a voiceless sound /θ/, while, with the second word, you should feel some vibration in your voice box as you begin to say /ð/. The small grammatical words of English which are spelt with a 'th' usually have the voiced /ð/. Many other words spelt 'th' often contain the voiceless /θ/.

Presence and absence of voice is also important in other pairs of consonants. See if you can tell which is voiced and which is voiceless in the following pairs:

/p/:/b/   /t/:/d/   /k/:/g/
/f/:/v/   /θ/:/ð/   /s/:/z/   /ʃ/:/ʒ/   /tʃ/:/ʤ/

Speakers from the South-West may have some difficulty here, as, for them, some of these pairs are not
distinguished, with both consonants being voiced. For
example, in literary representations of accents, *farmer*
might be spelt *varmer* to represent a South Western
accent. In RP, only the second of the consonants in
the pairs is voiced.

Another symbol which is usually represented by two
letters is long 's' /ʃ/, usually spelt 'sh'. You need to be
aware that, although two letters are often used in
spelling, there is only one sound. /ʃ/ is paired with its
voiced equivalent long 'z' /ʒ/, as in *measure*. Check
that you use the long symbols for these and not the
normal-sized ones. Some linguists use /š/ and /ž/.

The /ʃ/ and /ʒ/ symbols also occur in the combinations
/tʃ/ and /ʤ/. /tʃ/ is often spelt 'ch'. /ʤ/ is often spelt
'dge' but can sometimes be represented by 'j' or 'g', as
in *Jack* and *gin* respectively. Sounds which were
originally /ʒ/ often end up in English as /ʤ/, since /ʒ/ is
a relatively new sound which came from French. An
example of /ʒ/ becoming /ʤ/ can be seen in some
people's pronunciation of the end of the word *garage*
/gærɪʤ/.

Care must also be taken with long 'n' /ŋ/. It is also a
fairly new sound in English, and never occurs in an
initial position in a word. This is probably because it
originated as a variant of /n/ near /g/, and /ng/ is not a
possible initial cluster in English. What seems to have
happened is that /n/ became /ŋ/ near /g/ and then the
/g/ was lost, hence the origin of the term 'dropping the
g'. With the word *sing*, for instance, the change would
have been from /sɪng/ to /sɪŋg/ to /sɪŋ/. Some varieties
in the West and Midlands still keep /sɪŋg/. Other

varieties seem to have taken the process a stage further and have also lost the velar quality, in the back of the throat, of the /ŋ/ in some situations. This process seems to be confined only to -*ing* endings which are added on to words; for example, *singing* as /sɪŋɪn/ but *sing* as /sɪŋ/. Prescription may have played some part in slowing down this sound change. People also refer to the use of /sɪŋɪn/ for RP /sɪŋɪŋ/ as 'dropping the g', but what has happened in phonetic terms is that /ŋ/ has become /n/ – no /g/ is involved at all. Conservative RP speakers (the huntin', shootin' and fishin' brigade) also use /n/ for /ŋ/.

Finally, check that you have the right symbol for 'r'. The main problem with 'r', however, is that it is often there in spelling but not in pronunciation. This is especially so after a vowel (post-vocalically). In RP, no /r/ is pronounced in *bard*, *board*, *bird*, *beer*, *bear* and *cure*. Several centuries ago, when spelling was standardised, the 'r' would have been pronounced, but since then it has been lost and the preceding vowel has been lengthened to compensate. Some accents, notably Scots and some varieties of American English, retain this post-vocalic /r/, which means that the preceding vowels are also sometimes different from RP. Many Scots, for example, would pronounce *bard* as /bard/. Check your transcription to ensure that an /r/ is indeed present in the recording and that you have used the correct symbol for the preceding sound.

2   Check that you have used familiar symbols correctly.

(a)   Note the shape of the 'a'. Round 'ɑ' is used for the long vowel /ɑ:/, whereas curly 'a' occurs as the first element in the ash symbol /æ/ and with the diphthongs /aɪ/ and /aʊ/.

(b)   Notice that with 'i' the long vowel and the short vowel are also different shapes. The long vowel has a dotted 'i' /i:/ and the short vowel has a small capital 'i' /ɪ/. Again, check that you have used the right one.

(c)   There is a similar difference between the two 'u's. The long vowel is the normal 'u' /u:/, while the short one is curly 'u' /ʊ/. Check that these have also been used in the right positions. This is not always easy for speakers of Northern varieties, as they may have no distinction between /u:/ and /ʊ/. For example, some speakers in the North-East have no /ʊ/ and use /u:/ in words such as *book* and *cook*, while many RP speakers would use /ʊ/. In contrast, some Scots have no /u:/ and use /ʊ/ in words such as *pool* where an RP speaker would use /u:/.

(d)   Many consonants are familiar but are used in a different way from normal spelling.

There is no consonant /c/. /k/ is always used for the sound at the beginning of words such as *cat* as well as *kitchen* whether the sound is spelt 'k' or 'c' or in any other way. There is no /q/, as the spelling 'qu' usually represents the sound /kw/. For example, *queen* is /kwi:n/ in RP. Remember that 'c' might also represent /s/, as in *nice* which also has a silent 'e'. Check 'k's, 'c's and 'q's, and look out for silent letters.

The final symbol which might cause problems is /j/. This symbol is used for a sound often spelt with a 'y' in English, as in *yacht*, although in many European countries a 'j' spelling is used. /y/ in phonetics is reserved for the sound in the middle of the French word *lune* for *moon*, which is a cross between /i:/ and /u:/. /y/ is /i:/ said with rounded lips.

Exercise 8

Before proceeding, jot down any ideas that you had while you were transcribing which may be useful for your analysis. These ideas could also help you to decide what to look out for while you are reading around the subject, which is the topic of the next chapter.

8

Wider reading

All good A level students should already have been doing some background reading while studying various topics and different varieties of English during their course. One of the problems, however, with this relatively new subject is that, with a few exceptions, most of the books on the market have been produced for higher education students and are too difficult for A level students. You therefore need to develop a variety of searching and reading techniques.

Look for a book list (bibliography) at the back of any course book that you have been using. Pick out and note down any titles which seem relevant to your topic. The best way to note down details is to start with the details of the author(s), followed by the date of publication and the publisher. There are different ways of laying out these details but an acceptable way is as follows:

O'Donnell, W.R. and Todd, L. (1980) <u>Variety in Contemporary English</u> London: Allen and Unwin

You need to follow the layout, punctuation and underlining of this example consistently. Book titles are usually italicised in printed material but underlining is used in the example above as italics may not be available to students.

When you have noted down the details of all the relevant books, look in the catalogue of the school or college or town library for the classification number and then on the shelves. If a book is not in stock, the librarian might even be prepared to buy a new copy of the book, if it is in demand. However, you need to allow plenty of time for this. Search the shelves for any other promising books. Ask your teacher or lecturer to recommend any which may be suitable.

When you have found some promising books, search through them using the contents list and the index, if there is one. Dip into any chapters, sections or headings which seem relevant. Skim read any parts which seem irrelevant or too difficult. Note down anything useful, making sure that you know which books your notes are from. If you copy down exact words for quotation, also jot down the page number.

A good idea, especially if you intend going into higher education, is to obtain some sort of small box which will take cards of about postcard size. If you find any useful books, copy down the details of the book on one side of the postcard and summarise anything useful on the other side of the card. If you store these cards in alphabetical order in your 'index' box, you will have a ready-made bibliography (an alphabetical list of books consulted) which can be easily added to and then used at the end of your project. If you can't find a box, an elastic band will do.

Don't forget that periodicals and journals might be useful too. A relatively new and reasonably accessible quarterly review is English Today (abbreviated as ET). Articles from books and periodicals are laid out using quotation marks as follows:

Dubin, Fraida (1987) 'Answering machines' ET 10. 28–30

Here, 10 refers to the volume number and 28–30 to the page numbers. In printed material, the name of the publication is usually italicised and the volume number is usually printed in bold. Neither are used in the above example as students may not have access to them.

Television and radio programmes are another useful source of information. The BBC programme 'The Story of English' in nine parts contains useful information on many varieties of English. There is also a book to go with the series. You might find other useful books in the bibliographies of projects and at the end of this book.

When writing your project, you must acknowledge any ideas taken from other sources. It is customary to refer to the books by using the surname of the author(s) and the date of publication. If possible, you should also mention the page number, as in the following examples which could appear in a project:

> Trudgill and Hannah (1985:5) claim that the English in Bermuda is more like American English, while that spoken in the Falkland Islands is more like English English.

> Hughes and Trudgill (1979:31) point out that Scots, Irish and most North American accents have post-vocalic /r/.

> In Crystal and Davy (1969), style is said to vary according to the individual, the dialect, the time, the medium, how many participate, the nature of the task, the status of the participants, the mood and other singular features.

If you quote word for word from a book, you must use quotation marks. A long quotation should be started on a new line and indented, although a short quotation can be continued on the same line, as illustrated by the following examples:

> Freeborn (1986:84) notes that 'people's negative reactions' to accents are really only 'social prejudice'. He is confident that:
> > 'An objective study of accent can help to modify the instant reaction that we all tend to have towards an accent which is marked as socially inferior.'

Projects, however, are meant to be original, so beware of depending too much on what other people write. You should need no more than the occasional reference or two to other books. If you are studying a variety about which little or nothing has been written, then it is likely that you won't need to mention other authors at all. You must take care not to regurgitate what you read: test and apply information gained from books. Do not set about just trying to mention as many authors as you can to show how learned you are. Whatever you mention, it must be relevant to the task in hand and the citation should arise naturally. If you do discuss any books in the body of your project, you should list them in alphabetical order at the end of your project in a bibliography, in the same way as in the projects in Chapter 15 of this book.

Exercise 1

Keep reading around the subject and jot down any comments which could be useful to you, noting the source.

9

Organising the write-up

Now that you have decided on your topic, have collected your written or spoken material, and have completed your transcription, you are in a position to start writing up your project in earnest. Your examination syllabus may not suggest a format for your final project but you will need to organise your finished product in some way. A good guide on how to organise such a large task is given in the University of London syllabus. It is suggested that your project should be presented in the following five sections:

- Introduction
- Description
- Transcription or Material
- Analysis
- Evaluation

A book list (bibliography) or any appendices (additional information) required would be added to the end of this. Obviously, if your syllabus suggests a format such as this, you need to follow it closely and present your work under the five suggested headings. Even if your syllabus suggests a long essay, it is a good idea to divide up your work, mentally at least, into manageable sections. If you are familiar with a traditional report-type layout, you could use this format for organising your project, although you may not want to use these exact headings:

I   Terms of reference (indicating area and scope of study)

II   Introduction (background to the subject which may be linked with I)
III   Procedure (methods used to gather information)
IV   Findings (in various sections)
V   Conclusions (a summary leading to suggestions and re-commendations which may be given in another section in order to keep facts separate from opinions; however, this tends to be repetitive in a language project with a word limit)

A lengthy piece of work such as a project is much easier to read if it is written up with headings and subheadings. Such a layout looks more attractive than a continuous piece of writing, even if this is well paragraphed. However, if your syllabus suggests an essay format, this might indicate that headings and subheadings are not wanted, so you should check with your examination board.

Exercise 1

If your examination board does not suggest a format for your report, draw up a preliminary plan of the sections you are going to use.

10

A rough introduction

You did the groundwork for this section of your project when you decided on your reasons for studying a topic and thought about your aims. In addition, while you were transcribing your spoken material or looking over your written material, you will have gained some idea of the areas in which some interesting features occurred. What you need to do now is to put this information together in the form of a few paragraphs. An important consideration from the outset is to convey interest and enthusiasm about your project. The introduction need not be long. In fact, it is often better if it is brief and succinct, so that you can quickly get down to the meat of the project – the analysis.

A student studying child language, as in the selective phonetic transcription on page 71, might write the following introduction:

The language of a two-year-old

Introduction (Mark 1)
From the moment I studied child language acquisition, I became fascinated by the rate at which children acquire their mother tongues, which are such complex structures. Babies come into the world unable to speak but, after a few years, without any overt teaching, they are able to convey quite subtle meanings and produce an infinite number of sentences, many of which they have never heard before.

My enthusiasm for this area was further fuelled because I have a personal interest in child language acquisition. I have a two-year-old niece who is in the process of learning English. Moreover, a study of child language acquisition would be useful for my intended future career as a speech therapist.

In my project, I intend to focus on several areas of study. I will look at the pronunciation, vocabulary, grammar and conversational skills of my two-year-old niece. Then I will examine how her mother uses language when talking to her and whether this might facilitate her learning. I also hope to investigate how far my niece has followed the normal pattern of sound acquisition, as suggested in Crystal (1976) *Child Language, Learning and Linguistics*, and how far her grammatical and lexical acquisition is like that of other two-year-olds, as described in Brown (1973) *A First Language: The Early Stages* and de Villiers (1979) *Early Language*.

In her introduction the student could have mentioned some theories of language acquisition in passing. The 'innate theory' or the 'imitation theory' spring to mind. However, these would only be especially relevant if her material was going to be used to prove or disprove either or both of these theories, which may be difficult since the project involves only one child. Since the student intended to focus on the developmental aspects of child language acquisition, it is sufficient for her to mention briefly only some relevant background information in that area.

Introductions along similar lines to this one could be written for the projects mentioned in the earlier chapters of this book using the information provided. You must, however, regard your introduction at this stage as a first draft only, as your aims may change slightly during your detailed analysis. You may find, for instance, that you do not have enough information on, say, vocabulary but that the information on, say, pronunciation and grammar is more than sufficient for the required word length.

One of the major problems with projects is that students often have very wide and disparate aims. Do not feel that you have to discuss exhaustively every feature of your material, whether it is significant or not. The student studying child language acquisition in her niece might, for instance, find that there is far too much material to do justice to all of her aims in a word limit which usually works out at around 3000 words. She might therefore decide to narrow her focus of study as the project proceeds and concentrate on the child with no mention of the mother. She might also discover that the individual differences between two-year-olds in the literature are so great that they are of little help in determining the level of acquisition to be expected at that age. It is better to have a narrow focus, provided that you discuss all of the significant features, and to study the material thoroughly than to have a wide focus and an unsatisfactory discussion of each area.

The student writing about the language of a two-year-old ended up with the following introduction, with an altered third paragraph and a sentence added to the end of the first paragraph:

The language of a two-year-old

Introduction (Mark 2)

From the moment I studied child language acquisition, I became fascinated by the rate at which children acquire their mother tongues, which are such complex structures. Babies come into the world unable to speak but, after a few years, without any overt teaching, they are able to convey quite subtle meanings and produce an infinite number of sentences, many of which they have never heard before. This has led some linguists to believe that children are born with an innate capacity to learn language and, although the language environment plays a part, children do not just imitate what they hear.

My enthusiasm for this area was further fuelled because I have a personal interest in child language acquisition. I have a two-year-old niece who is in the process of learning English. Moreover, a study of child language acquisition would be useful for my intended future career as a speech therapist.

In my project, I intend to look at the pronunciation, vocabulary, grammar and conversational skills of my two-year-old niece. I hope to investigate how far my niece has followed the expected order of acquisition suggested in Crystal (1976) *Child Language, Learning and Linguistics.*

In contrast to this student who narrowed her focus, you might decide to widen your aims because you come across something interesting that you had not spotted at an early stage. However, you must take care not to stray too far from the subject of your title. For instance, if your area of study involves an accent and dialect, there is not much point including information on non-fluency features which are not specifically accental or dialectal but occur in most varieties of spontaneous spoken English. This would probably suggest to the examiner or moderator that you had run out of material and were padding out your project in the hope of reaching the required minimum length.

In either case, narrowing or widening your aims, you may want to rewrite your introduction after you have done your analysis. Alternatively, you could indicate this in your evaluation by noting that your original aims were too broad or that unexpected features came to light which you could not ignore.

Further examples of introductions can be seen in the projects in Chapter 15.

Exercise 1

Write a rough introduction to your project along the lines suggested here using any notes from the paragraph that you wrote at the end of Chapter 5.

11
The description of material

As with the introduction, this section of your project need not be long. Your description should include details of the context of the recording or written material. It can be tackled by asking yourself some *wh*-questions about your material. The following questions might be of use:

- Who?
- Where?
- How?
- What?
- When?

'Why' has generally been dealt with in the introduction. Any other background information necessary can also be included here. Examples of four descriptions are given in this chapter as illustrations.

A typical description of the material given in the detailed phonetic transcription on page 73 might read as follows:

The language of a north-east club comedian
Description
The material for this project is taken from a long playing (LP) record which was recorded in 1979 and is called 'Bobby Thompson: The Little Waster'. Bobby Thompson, whose nickname was 'The Little Waster', was a well-known comedian in the North-East of England. He was born in County Durham but lived in the Newcastle-upon-Tyne area. A map showing the area is included (see Figure 2).

Figure 2 *A map showing NE England*

Bobby Thompson's humour is based on the language and lives of working class people in the North-East of England. The LP record was recorded live in a North-East club. In the transcription, Bobby Thompson makes fun of the Royal Family and other important people such as General Montgomery.

A description of the material used in the general prosodic transcription on page 48 might look like this:

Unscripted commentary

Description

My transcription consists of a three and a half minute recording of two football matches played on 19 September 1987. The first match on tape is Everton versus Manchester United and features commentary by Alan Green backed up by Dennis Law who, as an ex-professional footballer, is more of a summariser than a commentator. Both men feature on Radio Two's 'Sport on Two' programme.

The second match features Brighton and Hove Albion against Sunderland with commentary by Bill Arthur from Metro Radio's 'Metro Sport' programme. Metro Radio is a local commercial radio station based in Newcastle-upon-Tyne in the North-East of England.

In order to select an interesting piece of recording to study, I had to edit a larger piece of tape to obtain two shorter recordings. Each part of the transcription, based on the recordings, features a goal being scored under controversial circumstances. Thus, on occasion, crowd noise makes it a little difficult to hear the commentators speak. This also created some problems in distinguishing a pause from a pause accompanied by an intake of breath.

The following description could accompany the transcription of the spontaneous monologue on page 35, to which phonetic symbols would need to be added if comments were going to be made about accent features.

The Washington accent and dialect

Description

The recording for this project took place in my home. Originally, I had planned for the recording to take the form of a conversation between a friend and myself. However, problems arose, such as the failure to maintain spontaneity and 'natural' dialect, mainly caused by the presence of the tape recorder.

Since I did not wish to study social interaction, only accent and dialect, I decided to adjust the situation to that of an interview, my friend taking the part of the interviewer, with me the interviewee. This did not work very well either, as my friend was merely asking questions in a Standard English dialect.

The best solution was to record me on my own talking about myself as spontaneously as possible. The recording therefore involves a four-minute monologue which has been transcribed in conventional spelling for the purpose of dialect study. It is accompanied by two extracts in phonetic script for the purpose of accent study.

I am an 18-year-old male of working class background who has always lived in the new town of Washington in Tyne and Wear, North-East England. The town contains some new industries and is based on what was originally an old Durham mining village. It is situated to the south of Newcastle-upon-Tyne and just to the north and west of Sunderland, which is on the River Wear. The inhabitants have therefore probably been influenced by the accents and dialects of both Newcastle and Sunderland, as well as County Durham, as Washington was originally part of that county. I hope to be able to detect all these strands in the analysis of my own speech.

A final description briefly outlines the collection of some written data:

Newspeak

Description

While skimming through a range of newspapers last June, I came across a topic which appeared to be treated very differently by different newspapers. This did not seem to be only a question of point of view but also of style. The topic involved was the eviction of hippies from around Stonehenge by police. Stonehenge is a pre-historic stone circle in Wiltshire, England. It had been customary for Druids (ancient Celtic priests) to celebrate the summer solstice there on Midsummer's Eve. Recently, this custom has been revived and local residents and conservationists have become worried about damage to the area. The four articles chosen for my study are taken from the English version of the Russian newspaper, *Pravda*, the *Sunday Mirror* and the *Daily Mirror* and a local paper, the *Yorkshire Evening Press*. It was important to retain the exact layout of these articles, so permission to take photocopies was obtained and these are included in the project.

Exercise 1

You should now be able to write a description of your own material before going on to the analysis, which is the subject of the next chapter. Don't forget to keep discussing first drafts of sections of your project with your teacher or lecturer, if you think this is necessary. If you are studying in a class situation, you may also want to pair up with a talk partner in your class and to become involved in small group or class discussions about each other's projects. This will enable you to talk through problems and clarify your thoughts. In this way, many more ideas will emerge than if you were working in isolation, although you must remember that this is an individual project.

12
The analysis

The need for good organisation has already been stressed, as we have gone through the introduction, the description and the transcription or copying of material for your project. Organisation is especially important in the analysis, which is the longest section.

12.1   Paragraph structure

A good tip for paragraph structure is to think of each paragraph roughly in terms of four points:

1   *Comment*: Make a comment about the feature you are going to discuss.
2   *Define*: Where necessary, employ accurate terminology and describe what you mean by the use of any terms, especially those which are less obvious.
3   *Quote*: Always give one or more examples of what you are discussing from your project. It is not enough just to give line numbers: you must quote the actual words as well, unless of course very large numbers of words are involved. Both line numbers and quotations are important as the examiner is likely to become exasperated if a lot of time has to be spent trying to verify a particular example in your material.
4   *Explain*: A good candidate thinks deeply about the material and is often able to give further explanations of, or reasons for, the occurrence of a particular feature.

A typical paragraph structure involving one feature associated with the spontaneous and dialect nature of the transcription of the monologue on page 35 might look as follows:

Pause fillers

One feature of this transcription which is typical of unplanned spoken English is the use of pause fillers. As the name suggests, pause fillers are words which fill what would otherwise be pauses in speech. They keep the speech going, although they do not contribute much to the meaning of the speech and would be omitted in edited written versions. A couple of examples of localised pause fillers are the uses of *wey* /weɪ/ in line 1 and *like* in line 2:

> [*wey*] I['ve] lived at
> Washington all my life *like* erm
> (.) at four different places (.h)

wey is a typical North-East of England pause filler equivalent to *wel!* whose function is to mark the initiation of a piece of speech. *like* is similar but marks the end of a particular piece of utterance. These words are not used in such functions in many other regions of England. Here, the speaker uses *wey* to indicate that he is starting; he uses *like* to give him more time to think about what to say next as he approaches the end of a sentence. If he had paused instead of using *wey* and *like erm* respectively, then the pauses would have been so long that it would have been embarrassing or would have indicated that the speaker wasn't going to start or had finished speaking.

The first sentence of this paragraph constitutes an initial comment. The next two sentences involve brief definitions and descriptions of pause fillers. The following sentence introduces two examples with line numbers and quotation. The remainder of the paragraph gives a more detailed explanation of the particular pause fillers *wey* and *like* in the transcription. Such a paragraph structure is a useful framework to bear in mind for your analysis.

12.2 Subsections

The importance of dividing your work into sections and subsections, unless your syllabus says otherwise, has already been mentioned. The analysis, which contains the meat of your project, is the longest section and should be divided up into subsections so that it looks well organised and is easy to read.

The subsections you use will of course depend on your material. You may have spotted obvious subsections, but if you haven't, or if you want to check systematically that you haven't missed anything significant, then a useful way of dividing up your analysis is into the various levels of language. You will probably already be used to organising essays involving textual analysis in this way. More detailed ideas of the types of subsection which arise from an examination of different sorts of material can be found in Section 12.3.

12.2.1 Sound

Language is a system of interrelated levels. The level which consists of the smallest language unit is sound, if the language is spoken. The technical words used when referring to pronunciation are phonetics (a detailed representation of sounds without regard to their use in a system) and phonology (a fairly broad transcription in which many sounds are idealised to some extent to show the balance and contrast typical of a sound system). As already mentioned, you will probably not need to become too involved in the difference between phonetics and phonology at A level, although you will need to know something about vowels (short and long monophthongs and diphthongs) and consonants which make up the syllables, the next largest unit, whose structure may also be a relevant feature in your material. If you are studying child language, for example, then you could find that, in the early stages of acquisition, all syllables have a consonant vowel (CV) structure and that CC structures or syllables beginning with V are rare.

Other features which could be included in a subsection on sound are non-fluency features such as hesitation and recycling. Note, however, that some non-fluency features, such as tortuous syntax and long or incomplete sentences, are grammatical rather than sound features. Non-fluency probably straddles most of the language levels.

Prosodics, which includes volume, speed, rhythm, pitch and such like, could also be discussed in a sound subsection. Material with a literary feel may exploit devices such as alliteration (repetition of initial consonants), assonance (repetition of vowel sounds), onomatopoeia (words which sound like what they represent, for example, *buzz*) and rhyme. Advertisements are also well known for using these devices to attract attention.

A useful reference book on pronunciation is Gimson (1980). Hughes and Trudgill (1979) and Trudgill and Hannah (1985) contain comments on a variety of accents. Crystal and Davy (1969) outline prosodic features.

Exercise 1

Make a rough start by analysing your project material to see if it has any interesting or significant sound features. If it does, then write a few paragraphs using suitable headings for sub-subsections which may include some of the terms mentioned here. If the sound features are not the most important, you may want to start with another level of language.

12.2.2   Graphology
This is a useful cover-all term from Crystal and Davy (1969). It can be used to discuss most aspects of spelling, punctuation and layout. Handwriting, spelling and punctuation can also be called orthography. If your project is based on spoken material, then the letters and spelling will be largely unimportant, although there may be the odd occasion when you want to point out the relationship between spoken and written symbols. With written data, on the other hand, there could be quite a bit to say about the graphology. For instance, legal material is well known for sparse punctuation, for initial decorated letters and for the unusual use of capitals. Advertisements may attract attention with unconventional spellings such as *skool*. Historical passages may have inconsistent spellings or symbols such as the thorn (originally þ) which is no longer in use. A useful convention for indicating letters in spelling is the use of

diamond brackets ⟨þ⟩. This helps to differentiate letters and sounds.

Novels sometimes have characters whose accents are indicated in unconventional orthography. On the other hand, unconventional spellings such as *wot* do not really indicate accent: they could show that a character is uneducated or that what is being said is informal.

Newspapers use columns and short paragraphs for ease of reading. Large, bold headlines in capital letters attract attention. The decreasing size of the type leads the eye gently into the article. You should be alert for any of these graphological devices used in your material.

Exercise 2

If there are any significant or interesting graphological features in your project material, write some paragraphs on them. (This applies only if you are studying written material.)

12.2.3 Vocabulary

Sounds or letters and syllables make up the vocabulary or lexis of a language. It will probably be worth examining the words in your material to see if they display any significant features. The multi-volume OED (*Oxford English Dictionary*) and its supplements could be useful here. The two-volume compact edition with its magnifying glass is exactly the same. Recently, the *New Oxford English Dictionary* has been published. In this, the OED has been integrated with its supplements and new material has been added. In addition, the original pronunciation system has been replaced by the symbols of the International Phonetic Association. The dictionary is also available on computer disk, which allows searches to be made. Such dictionaries will tell you, among other things, when any significant vocabulary items in your project material were first spotted in writing, which language they were adopted from, how they have changed in meaning, and whether they are obsolete, archaic, colloquial, dialectal and such like.

You may discover, for example, that much of the vocabulary

in your transcription is polysyllabic and Latinate, giving a formal tone to the material. Remember, however, that not all polysyllabic words are learned, that dictionaries take a long time to write, and that often your own intuitions may be more up to date.

In addition to dictionaries which give you the etymology of a word, there are also dialect dictionaries and dictionaries of slang, colloquialisms, idioms, catch-phrases, Americanisms, scientific and technological words, and so on. West's (1953) *A General Service List of English Words* will give you a rough idea of whether vocabulary items are common or infrequent, although the situation may have changed a little since the list was first compiled. The age of books is something that you must be aware of when reading around the subject. You should try to obtain the latest editions where possible, although school or college or town libraries sometimes have older editions which can provide valuable information.

Breaking up any interesting words into their smallest meaningful units of language (morphemes) will show how they have been formed. There are many different patterns of word formation. Affixes, compounds, acronyms, shortened words, blends and conversions can be seen in the following examples: *micro-fined, hospitalise, take-away, NATO, ad, brunch, a must*. A summary of word formation can be found in Quirk and Greenbaum (1973). Fromkin and Rodman (1983) has short sections on word coinage and loan words borrowed from other languages. Sometimes words are nonce formations which are coined for a particular occasion, appear a few times and then are lost. An example of a nonce word is *orangemostiest*. True inventions such as *Omo*, an old brand name for a washing powder, are rare. You will need to say what such words contribute to the overall feel of your material. A useful reference book is Carter (1987) *Vocabulary*.

Exercise 3

Examine the vocabulary in your project material and, if there is anything significant, roughly write one or more subsections on it.

12.2.4 Grammar

The next level of language is known as the grammar of the language. This is where words are made into sentences. The system of rules governing the construction of sentences is known as syntax. This involves putting the words in a certain order.

Grammar involves not only the ordering of words but the placing of 'small' words (function or grammatical words) between the main or lexical words in the sentence to link them together. Function or grammatical words are the ones that you would miss out when writing a telegram (for example, *and*, *at*, *a* and so on).

Making words into sentences also involves adding endings to words. Grammatical endings are called inflections. This is part of the morphology of the language, just like the study of affixes in word formation is. An example of an inflection is the *-s* for the plural in *cats* or the *-ed* for past tense in some uses of *kicked*. There may be something unusual about the inflections in your transcription, especially if your material is dialectal.

Grammar also involves the study of word class patterns. Lexical words include the following word classes: nouns, verbs, adjectives and adverbs. It may be worthwhile, for example, examining the type of noun or the structure of the groups or phrases with nouns and verbs. The noun phrases may be mainly simple and concrete, or complex and abstract with lots of pre- and post-modification. You will need to explain the reasons for this. Conjunctions, auxiliary verbs, pronouns, articles, prepositions and such like are function words. There may be something significant to discuss about these in your project material.

The sentence structure in your project material might be simple, compound, complex, compound–complex or even minor (because it is incomplete), as illustrated by the following examples:

John entered the room   (*simple*)

John entered the room and sat at the table   (*compound*)

After John entered the room, he sat at the table   (*complex*)

After John entered the room, he sat at the table and went to sleep   (*compound–complex*)

Kicks the ball to the far side   (*minor*)

The structure of sentences and clauses can also be analysed in terms of subjects, predicators, objects, complements and adverbials, as in the following sentence:

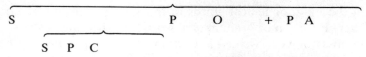

John, who was Mary's cousin, entered the room and sat at the table

The subject in this sentence is complex because a relative clause, *who was Mary's cousin*, is embedded within it.

There may be something significant to say about, for example, the number and placement of adverbials in your material. Sentence type may be important. There may be reasons for the frequency of occurrence of declaratives, interrogatives or imperatives.

When analysing spoken material, you should remember that sentence elements may be missing; indeed, it may not be possible to analyse the utterances in terms of sentences at all. Speech often has non-fluency or merged syntax and occurs in information or tone units which may be more important than sentences.

A useful tip when looking at grammar is to imagine a basic sentence with subject, predicator and object, as in 'Boy meets girl'. This sentence can then be made more complicated in various ways: by changing the verb, by putting something in front of or after the noun, by altering the order of the subject, predicator and object, or by adding additional phrases or clauses joined in particular ways. You may need to categorise the sentences or utterances in your project material and decide what their overall effect is on your material.

A useful grammatical reference book is Quirk *et al.* (1985) *A Comprehensive Grammar of the English Language*. The less detailed version, Quirk and Greenbaum (1973), is also helpful.

Other useful grammar books are Freeborn (1987) and (1984).

Exercise 4

A quick look at the categories referred to by the terms in this section will reveal whether there are any interesting grammatical features in your material. Don't forget to try to explain why they occur. Your analysis would be fairly dull if it was composed merely of comments such as: 'There are 101 adverbials in my transcription'. Write a few draft paragraphs on anything of grammatical interest in your project material.

12.2.5 Semantics

Semantics is the study of meaning in language. If you have not already discussed any features of meaning alongside the vocabulary in your analysis, you may need a separate subsection in which to do this.

If there is anything significant about the connotations of the words used, you will need to mention this. For example, it could be significant that a word such as *slim*, which has favourable connotations, is used rather than one such as *skinny*, which has unfavourable connotations, or *thin*, which is neutral.

Your material may involve ambiguity (double meaning) or polysemy (multiple meaning). This might be deliberate, as in punning, or inadvertent, as in the headline 'General flies back to front'. Punning often relies on homophony (two or more words which have the same sound). An example of homophony can be seen in the words *told* and *tolled* (both /təʊld/ in RP), hence the humour of: 'When he died, they told the sexton; and the sexton tolled the bell'. Exaggeration or understatement could also be employed in your project material for humorous purposes.

Synonyms (words with similar meanings) could occur in your project material. Legal language is full of pairs of near-synonyms such as *goods and chattels* or *breaking and entering*. They are said to have originated when French and English 'equivalents' were co-ordinated to prevent misunderstanding and to ensure inclusiveness. Thesauruses contain lists of synonyms. Comparisons in the form of similes, metaphors, images, symbols or personification could occur if your project has a literary flavour.

Your material could include uses which lead you to trace a change of meaning in terms of narrowing, broadening, weakening and such like. For instance, the use of *starving* to mean 'cold' in some dialects can be accounted for by the narrowing down of Old English uses of the word meaning 'dying' to 'dying slowly' to 'dying of cold'. Weakening would then result in *starving* meaning 'cold'. In Standard English, narrowing occurred in terms of 'dying of hunger', so weakening caused the meaning to become 'very hungry'.

Your project material might also contain significant antonyms (opposites), some contradictions and absurdities, or words from a few semantic fields only.

Some of the terms referred to here can be looked up in Palmer (1981) *Semantics*. If the meaning has changed, a useful book for reference is Stern (1965) *Meaning and Change of Meaning*. A simple outline of some aspects of meaning can be found in Chapters 16–18 of Tinkel (1988).

Exercise 5

Examine your project material for any interesting features of meaning and write a few draft paragraphs on anything important.

12.2.6 Discourse features
You may find that you come across important features to do with language use which do not fit into the sound, vocabulary, grammar and semantics already discussed. An obvious category which has not been mentioned is the structure of the whole discourse. Cohesion, for example, occurs because the material is a text or discourse consisting of many sentences or utterances – the material hangs together in some way. Narratives, for example, could be organised in terms of a story within a story or by using a flashback technique.

If your transcription involves dialogue, then the interaction between speakers may be important. You should be able to work out the relationships and relative status of the participants by various clues. You might need to study turn-taking to see if it is orderly or involves overlapping, interruptions or latching on. You may find that participants are invited to reply by being questioned, or that their contributions are completely unsolicited. One of the participants could continue to hold the floor by hardly taking a breath or by placing pauses in unusual places, rather than at the end of structures. Conversely, a speaker may just fade out, thereby allowing another person to start speaking.

A useful book is Wardhaugh (1985) *How Conversation Works*. Chapter 2 of McTear (1985) gives a useful framework, while Chapter 15 of Tinkel (1988) outlines discourse structure.

Exercise 6

Examine your material for anything interesting in terms of discourse structure and write a few rough paragraphs on it.

12.2.7 Some final advice

Some terms from the various levels of language description have been discussed in the previous subsections. These terms are by no means exhaustive: there may be other features of importance in your material which you can label and categorise yourself. Moreover, you should not necessarily expect to have sections on all of the levels outlined so far, and some sections will probably be much longer than others.

You can also expect to find that some features can have several alternative but equally valid explanations. The idea that there are grey and fuzzy areas, and that there is not always only one right and one wrong answer, is an important concept to be learned at A level. This phenomenon can be demonstrated in the following two extracts from a project about the language of a three-year-old child.

she do (2.0) she make a Christmas cake
can't do it

It is not clear in the first extract whether the child has not yet acquired the *-s* form for the third person singular present because she has not reached that stage of development or because her local dialect does not have it. Indeed, both explanations could be true, with one reinforcing the other. Similarly, in the second extract, it is not clear whether the child has omitted the subject pronoun because she is unsure of its use or because this is typical of informal speech, as adults often shorten sentences in this way when speaking informally.

When you come to do your analysis, you may decide not to organise your analysis in terms of the various levels of language. For example, you may choose to organise it in terms of the beginning, middle and end of the material, discussing language features from any of the levels in the appropriate section, or you may choose to organise by function rather than form. A variety of ways of organising your analysis can be seen in the next section. The most important thing is to look closely at your own material and to write about the interesting and significant things, rather than writing according to some preconceived section headings.

12.3   Examples of organisation

Examples of the subsections used in the analyses of the projects listed in Chapters 3 and 5 are given below. These have been listed in detail so that you can work out the content of the analyses. In many cases, they were grouped under broader headings in the actual project and organised more coherently in the final version.

Spoken topics
  1   *Airspeak*
      A.   Pronunciation
      B.   Vocabulary 1. Climb 2. Compass and clock words
            3. Cruise 4. Heading 5. LBA 6. Level 7. London

8. Maintain 9. Numbers 10. Polite words 11. Port and
starboard 12. Recleared 13. Report 14. Request
15. Roger 16. Route 17. Squawk 18. Standby one
19. Traffic

C. Grammar 1. Deletion a. Subject and predicator
b. *Flight Level* and the homophones *to/two* c. Other
deletions 2. Sentence types 3. Present participles

D. Dialogue features 1. Pauses 2. Pause fillers 3. Self-
correction 4. Turn-taking.

2 *The language of humour*
1. Voice quality 2. Accent 3. Word formation
4. Homophones 5. Polysemy 6. Understatement

3 *The language of a soap opera*
A. Dialect grammar 1. Plurals 2. *Never* as negative
3. Non-standard verb forms 4. Demonstratives
5. Prepositions
B. Lexis 1. Dialect vocabulary 2. Colloquial vocabulary
C. Pronunciation 1. Short vowels 2. Diphthongs
3. Consonants
D. Discourse features of scripted dialogue
E. Language differences between characters

4 *Sports commentary on local hospital radio*
1. Non-fluency 2. Vocabulary 3. Grammar 4. Point of view
5. Audience

5 *Motherese*
1. Introduction
2. Pronunciation a. Repetition of syllables
b. Replacement of sounds c. Onomatopoeia
d. Rhyme e. Diminutives f. Imitation of child
3. Intonation and stress a. Exaggerated rhythm
b. Exaggerated stress c. Exaggerated intonation
4. Vocabulary
5. Grammar a. Repetition of structures b. Frequent use
of questions c. Shortened sentences d. Replacement
of pronouns
6. Speaking for the child

6 *Nigerian pidgin*
a. Sound (i) Simplified and shortened vowels

       (ii) Stressing unstressed syllables (iii) Lack of /ð/ and /ə/ (iv) Reduction of clusters

  b.   Vocabulary (i) African names (ii) English words (iii) Others

  c.   Grammar (i) VPs with *Dohn*, *Go*, *Fit*, *Mek*, *De* (ii) Base forms (iii) 'Empty' *Na* (iv) The preposition *Foh* (v) Word order

7 *Male and female language*
1. Intonation and Pitch 2. Non-fluency features
3. Paralinguistic features – laughter 4. Standard and non-standard forms 5. RP and accent 6. Vocabulary
7. Intensifiers 8. Tag questions

8 *CB radio language*
  A.   Interaction 1. Turn-taking 2. Shared knowledge 3. Ending the conversation
  B.   Vocabulary 1. Break/breaker 2. Copy 3. Pick a window 4. Channel names 5. Handles 6. Eye on the side 7. Number formations 8. Non-standard lexis 9. The police
  C.   Grammatical structure 1. Repetition 2. Telegrammatic syntax 3. Sentence types

9 *The language of some students with learning difficulties and their teacher*
  A.   Teacher's language 1. Questioning 2. Prosodics 3. Repetition and expansion 4. Control of turn-taking 5. Encouraging words and sounds 6. Avoidance of pronouns
  B.   The students' language 1. Pronunciation 2. Vocabulary 3. Grammar 4. Turn-taking

10 *Political rhetoric*
1. Degree of fluency 2. Use of pauses 3. Stress and intonation 4. Alliteration 5. Accent 6. Type of vocabulary 7. Metaphors. 8. Favourable and unfavourable connotations 9. Repetition and parallelism 10. Personal pronouns 11. Modal verbs 12. Delaying the main point 13. Rhetorical questions

11 *The language of a chat show*
1. Initiating the interview 2. Phatic communion

3. Structure 4. Keeping the conversation going 5. Three-way conversation 6. Keeping the audience informed
7. Entertainment value 8. Modesty effects of guest
9. Degree of spontaneity 10. Overlaps and interruptions
11. Keeping to the topic 12. Elaboration 13. Abrupt changes of subject 14. Summing up 15. Termination of the interview

12 *A radio phone-in*
   A. First phone call 1. Putting caller at ease 2. Handling a delicate topic 3. Getting action 4. Accent of DJ and caller 5. Ending the phone call
   B. Second phone call 1. Fluency of DJ and caller 2. Humour 3. Age of caller 4. Ending the phone call

13 *Teacher talk*
   1. Greeting 2. Initiating topic 3. Structuring the lesson
   4. Foregrounding 5. Reprimands 6. Correcting
   7. Encouraging 8. Response from class 9. Status of participants 10. Assumed body language 11. Volume
   12. Fluency 13. Use of pauses and silence 14. Forms of address 15. Subject-specific vocabulary 16. Repetition
   17. Commands and requests 18. Types of questions

14 *A contrast between two accents*
   A. Long vowels 1. Shortening 2. Diphthongisation
   B. Short vowels 1. Opening 2. Centralisation
   C. Diphthongs 1. Monophthongisation 2. Other older uses
   D. Consonants 1. 'Dropping the g' 2. 'Dropping the h'

15 *Telephone techniques*
   1. Answering 2. Greeting 3. Explicitness 4. Degree of formality 5. Turn-taking 6. Voiced non-fluency
   7. Preparedness 8. Length and types of sentences
   9. Feedback 10. Semantic structure 11. Ending

16 *Time travel*
   1. Non-fluency features 2. Speed 3. Contractions
   4. Formality and informality of vocabulary
   5. Subordination 6. Other linguistic features

Written topics

1 *Chaucer's English*
   A. Orthography 1. Manuscript A (i) ⟨ŷ⟩ for ⟨i⟩ (ii) ⟨þ⟩ (iii)
      ⟨u⟩ and ⟨v⟩ (iv) ⟨I⟩ for ⟨J⟩ (v) Long ⟨ʃ⟩ (vi) Abbreviations
      (vii) Punctuation (viii)Variant spellings 2. Manuscript
      B (i) Final ⟨e⟩s, (ii) Doubling (iii) Pronunciation
   B. Vocabulary 1. Archaisms 2. Obsolete words
      3. Semantic change 4. French words 5. Idiom
   C. Grammar 1. Word order (i) Inversion of subject and
      predicator (ii) Thematic adverbials (iii) Object
      placement 2. Verbs (i) Present tense (*e*)*th* endings (ii)
      Past forms (iii) Impersonal uses 3. Negatives 4. Nouns
      5. Adjectives as adverbs

2 *Legal language*
   A. Graphology 1. Capitals 2. Gothic 3. Other punctuation
      4. Spacing
   B. Lexis 1. Archaisms 2. Formal vocabulary 3. French and
      Latin
   C. Syntax 1. Adverbials 2. Complex NPs 3. Co-ordination
      4. Asides 5. Relative clauses 6. Non-finite clauses
      7. Passive VPs 8. Demonstratives as determiners

3 *Newspeak*
   1. Selection of items 2. Placement 3. Layout
   4. Connotations and choice of vocabulary 5. Style
   6. Structure 7. Point of view

4 *Hopkins*
   1. Layout and structure 2. Metre 3. Alliteration 4. Rhyme
   5. Other techniques with sound 6. Word formation
   7. Deviant syntax 8. Meaning

Spoken and written topics

1 *The language of a seven-year-old*
   Spoken, read and written texts each discussed under these
   headings:
   1. Non-fluency
   2. Syllable structure (consonants and vowels)
   3. Vocabulary
   4. Grammar a. Noun phrases (i) Articles (ii) Pronouns

(iii) Pre-modifiers b. Prepositions c. Verbs d. Sentence structure (i) Interrogatives (ii) Vocatives

2 *Franglish*
1. Pronunciation a. Consonants b. Vowels c. Stress d. Pitch
2. Vocabulary a. French cognates b. French idioms c. Colloquialisms d. Overgeneralisation
3. Grammar a. Complex sentences b. Verbs (i) Omission of auxiliary verbs (ii) Present for past (iii) Lack of *-s* form c. Noun phrases (i) Omission of indefinite article (ii) Indirect objects without *to* (iii) Double comparative (iv) Unusual prepositions

3 *Advertising language*
1. Voice quality 2. Length of tone units 3. Variation in tone, speed and volume 4. Use of pauses 5. Alliteration 6. Punctuation, spelling and layout 7. Jingles 8. Images 9. Sensual vocabulary 10. French vocabulary 11. Scientific words 12. Neologisms 13. Imperatives 14. Repetitive structure 15. Superlatives and comparatives 16. Delayed subjects

4 *The language of religion*
1. Introduction
2. Biblical extract a. Archaic pronouns b. Religious lexis c. Verb inflections d. Loose co-ordination
3. Narrative a. Non-fluency b. Colloquial vocabulary c. Use of formulae d. Past tense
4. Prayer a. Rhythm and pace b. Vocatives c. Exclamations d. Pre- and post-modification e. NPs in apposition f. The subjunctive

5 *A study in story-telling*
1. Beginning the story 2. Chronology 3. Introduction of character 4. Dialogue 5. Use of accent and dialect 6. Digressions 7. Humour 8. Atmosphere 9. Contact with audience 10. Build-up and punch-line 11. Non-fluency 12. Rhythm, speed and pausing 13. Literary devices 14. Continuers to prevent interruption 15. Asides 16. Simplicity of VP 17. Sayings and clichés 18. Colloquial and slang vocabulary 19. Complexity of NP 20. Summary

21. Recapping 22. Concluding the story 23. After the story

6 *Parliamentary debate*
   1. Forms of address
   2. Fluency
   3. Turn-taking
   4. Vocabulary a. Favourable connotations
       b. Unfavourable connotations c. Word formation
       techniques d. Quotable phrases
   5. Pronouns
   6. Positives and negatives
   7. Sentence structure

7 *Style*
   1. Situation I a. Interaction b. Pronunciation
       c. Vocabulary d. Grammar
   2. Situation II a. Graphology b. Vocabulary c. Grammar
       and so on for each situation

The headings given here are meant as a guide only. You do not
need to use such detailed subheadings unless it is necessary.
However, a glance through the headings used will give you
some ideas about the content of the analyses in those projects
listed. You may then be able to ascertain more easily what the
important features in your analysis are.

Exercise 7

Look through the paragraphs you have written for your analysis, design suitable titles for your subsections, if you haven't
already done so, and reorganise or group them accordingly.

12.4   Unique pattern of organisation

There are several books available which put forward various
ways of analysing linguistic material (for example, Crystal and
Davy (1969) *Investigating English Style*). You might find these
books difficult if you are an A level student, but they are useful

as a starting point if you can persevere – they will give you plenty of good ideas about what to analyse.

Many students make the mistake of slavishly following any suggested method of analysis regardless of whether particular categories are important in their projects. For instance, there is no point in analysing the sentence structure of your material unless you have a 'hunch' that there is something significant to say about this: a preliminary glance may suggest a high proportion of complex sentences, which may add a learned tone to the material; conversely, most of the sentences could be simple or co-ordinated, which you might feel makes the material easier to understand.

A good project has a framework of analysis based on the project material itself rather than on some theoretical framework, only some of whose features may be significant. Conversely, you may find that there are significant features in your project material which are not covered in any suggested theoretical framework of analysis.

A good tip is to look for interesting and significant features in your project material first, rather than beginning with some preconceived framework which might not fit. This approach explains why the projects listed in the previous section have different headings in their analyses. The authors are merely responding to the different nature of their material and thus produce a unique pattern of headings in their analyses. Even projects on similar topics rarely have identical subheadings.

Exercise 8

Check that you have included everything interesting and significant from your material in your analysis. If you have included anything insignificant, look at it again and decide whether to abandon it. Group similar features to improve coherence.

12.5   Presentation of findings

It has already been suggested in Chapter 8 that if you quote word for word from a book, you must use quotation marks. Quotation marks can also be used for quoting sections from your own material. Like quotations taken from books, longer sections should be started on a new line and indented. Shorter quoted sections, consisting of only a few words, can be continued on the same line as the comments made about them. However, it is not usual to use quotation marks when discussing only a word or phrase. The words cited are usually italicised, or underlined if this facility is not available. This makes them easier to pick out from the comments made about them. If you gloss (that is, give the meaning of any words), then this is the time to use quotation marks. Italics (or underlining) and quotation marks are used as follows:

Slim basically means 'thin' but has favourable connotations.

Your work will be easier to read if you adopt this style of layout.

Some findings can be enhanced if presented in other than

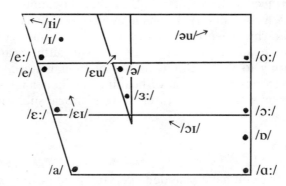

Long vowels		Short vowels		Diphthongs	
/e:/	pay	/ɪ/	bid	Arrow shows movement of sound	
/ɛ:/	there	/e/	bed	/ɪi/	see
/o:/	go	/a/	bad	/ɛɪ/	pie
/ɔ:/	board	/ɒ/	cod	/ɛu/	house
/ɑ:/	bard	/ə/	cup put	/əu/	shoe
/ɜ:/	bird			/ɔɪ/	boy

Figure 3 *Vowel chart of the Sunderland accent*

essay form. Graphical techniques such as tables, charts and diagrams can be adopted.

A vowel chart, as described on page 68, may be useful if your analysis involves the discussion of the pronunciation of vowels, as shown in Figure 3.

Maps can be useful in showing isophones or isoglosses (lines separating areas of the country with different pronunciations or vocabulary and grammatical items). An example is given in Figure 4.

Tables often allow significant findings to be seen at a glance. They also indicate that a thorough analysis of the material has been undertaken rather than a vague impressionistic approach. Tables 1 and 2 illustrate how they may be used.

Figure 4 *Isophones distinguishing Northern and Southern accents*

Table 1   The complexity of sentences of the three participants in the project

Clause	Grandmother	Daughter	Granddaughter
Relative clauses	8	4	1
Adverbial clauses			
time	1 ⎫	1 ⎫	1 ⎫
result	2 ⎬ 8	2 ⎬ 6	2 ⎬ 4
reason	3 ⎪	1 ⎪	0 ⎪
condition	2 ⎭	2 ⎭	1 ⎭
Total subordinate clauses	16	10	5

Table 2   Function words used at age 4 and 5

Function word	4-year-old	5-year-old
Pronouns	15	21
Prepositions	8	9
Conjunctions	7	12
Total	30	42

Tree diagrams, as illustrated in Figures 5 and 6, are useful when discussing grammatical features, where S = sentence, Cl = clause, NP = noun phrase, VP = verb phrase and Adj = adjective. Such tree diagrams might help you to make a claim about the complexity of the sentence structure in your project.

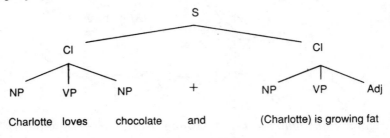

Figure 5   *Tree diagram of compound sentence*

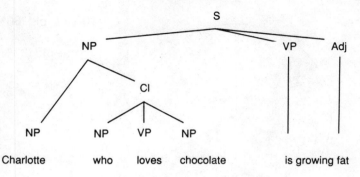

Figure 6   *Tree diagram showing embedding*

Pie charts and bar charts can also be useful when used appropriately, as exemplified by Figures 7 and 8.

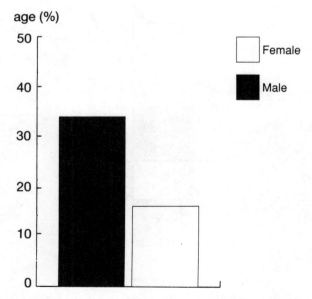

Figure 7   *Bar chart showing usage of imperative sentences by males and females*

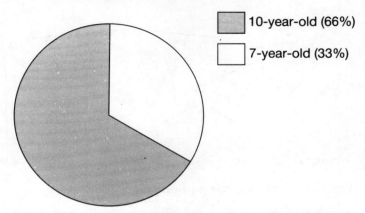

Figure 8   *Pie chart showing proportion of time that two speak-ers hold the floor in conversation*

You can also invent diagrams and charts of your own where necessary. Interesting ways of showing, for example, the amount of time that two participants speak in a conversation can be seen in Figures 9 and 10.

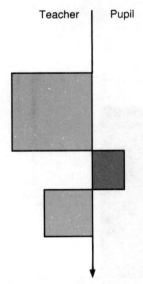

Figure 9   *Diagram showing teacher's and pupil's contribution to the conversation*

Line no.	Main speaker	Topic	Progress
1–12	Teacher	Exams	Initial topic has little success in involving pupil.
13–42	Teacher	Project	Change of subject eventually produces limited response from pupil.
43–60	Pupil	Project	Interest shown by pupil because of personal involvement.
61–89	Teacher	Holiday	Discourse redirected as pupil runs out of ideas. Taken up by teacher but not much by pupil.

Figure 10   *Chart showing the progress of conversation*

The chart in Figure 11 summarises information about the grammar of a particular dialect.

Grammatical feature	Dialect	Standard English	Comments
Nouns	year pound	years pounds	Zero plural for nouns of measurement from older English.
Verbs	I've rang he's took	I've rung he's taken	Past participle the same as past form for strong verbs which have fewer forms than Standard English.
Negatives	You don't need no blazer for that fire. I haven't had no dinner yet.	You don't need a blazer for that fire. I haven't had any dinner yet.	Double negative – negative put in all possible places to ensure that the negative is not missed. Standard English negative marked once on the verb.

Figure 11   *Summary of grammatical features of the dialect appearing in the transcription*

Sometimes lists such as these, if they are long, are better in an appendix (appendices if there is more than one) at the end of the project. However, there is no doubt that graphical representations can enhance your presentation in the body of your project.

Exercise 9

Look through your material and see if you could usefully
enhance your presentation using graphical techniques.

Exercise 10 [*Summary exercise*]

Scour your material for interesting and significant features.
You should come up with a number of headings that you can
use. Write these up using the paragraph structure suggested in
Section 12.1. Remember that sometimes your material will be
enhanced if it is also presented with illustrative diagrams,
charts, tables and such like. Follow the style of italicising or
underlining cited words, quoting examples and glossing meaning with single sets of quotation marks. A glance through the
analysis sections of the completed projects in Chapter 15 will
help you before you start writing up a final version of your
analysis.

13
The evaluation

The evaluation or conclusion, like the introduction and description to your project, will generally be a fairly brief section. In it, you will probably want to summarise your findings and give an honest, objective assessment of your work and the insights you have gained.

You may be pleased that you have discovered the distinctive features of a hitherto unstudied variety of English, or that you have proved or disproved theories put forward by other linguists and researchers. On the other hand, you could be disappointed that the features that you had intended to study did not occur to the extent that you had hoped and, as a consequence, you had to change your aims from those stated in your introduction. There is also the possibility that unexpected results will emerge. Maybe your soap opera or chat show was less like natural conversation than you had anticipated, or perhaps the variety of English that you were studying was more intricate and not as easy to produce as you had imagined. This often happens with unscripted commentaries or jokes or stories. You may also have come across some difficulties: when transcribing tones or phonetic symbols, finding clear sections on your tape, or searching for literature on your chosen topic. As a result of your study, you might want to make suggestions or recommendations. For instance, if you have discovered how adults can encourage child language learning, you could suggest strategies for parents; if you find out how a passage from a children's book could be altered to facilitate learning, you could draw up recommendations.

Your evaluation should show how your project has been a

learning experience in some way. A possible example of such an experience is learning for the first time how difficult it is to organise a lengthy piece of work so as to avoid repetition and to keep within the word limit. You may have been faced with the painful experience of having to reduce the number of words, or with the tedium of having to write and rewrite sections until they were polished. Since language is a system and a continuum, there are always fuzzy areas when categorising. You could therefore have found that placing linguistic features into particular sections was difficult. Overall though, you should be able to convey enthusiasm and the immense sense of achievement that you have felt in completing such a task.

A couple of examples of evaluations on similar topics now follow.

A contrast between two accents and dialects: Tyneside and Wearside

Evaluation
In this project, I have shown that the two accents and dialects that I have studied have many differences from RP and Standard English in all fields: pronunciation, vocabulary and grammar.

Most of the differences are in pronunciation, especially vowels, with two sounds in particular (that is, /ɪi/ and /əu/ rather than /i:/ and /u:/), showing that a speaker is not a Geordie. As far as consonants are concerned, Geordies do not seem to 'drop aitches' whereas Wearsiders often do.

The vocabulary of the two dialects is different from Standard English in the retention of older forms, some of which are also found in Scots English and American English. The main difference between the Wearsider and the Tynesider in the transcription was the use of *dinnet* by the former and *divvent* by the latter for the Standard English form *don't*.

With regard to grammar, considerable differences were found from Standard English in the patterning of irregular verbs; in personal, reflexive and relative pronouns; with number in nouns; as well as in the use of some prepositions and some adverbs.

My results lead me to conclude that accents and dialects are very much alive and kicking, despite claims to the contrary, and despite moves and influences towards standardisation. I have also dispelled the myth that anyone north of Leeds is a Geordie by showing the not inconsiderable differences between these two neighbouring varieties of North-East English: Tyneside and Wearside.

Both the sounds and the grammar of these North Eastern varieties were discovered to belong to systems which are just as rule governed as RP and Standard English. I therefore conclude that they are efficient as language systems and should not be proscribed against.

The Sunderland accent and dialect

Evaluation

I was a little disappointed with the results from this project. I had intended to study both the accent and the dialect of Sunderland and I chose an informant who seemed to be 'broad'. I made arrangements to record a discussion with him but in 30 minutes of recorded material, I could not find 3–5 minutes which had a lot of grammatical and lexical differences from Standard English, so the project became more of a study of the accent of Sunderland rather than its dialect as well.

If I were doing this project again, I would probably choose a less educated informant. My informant was probably more of a dialect speaker in his youth but went into higher education and also reads a lot. This may account for the relative standardisation of his dialect, although his accent remains very 'broad', which led me to expect more dialect features in his speech.

This study has shown me how difficult it is to capture dialectal differences in small amounts of speech. Any one sound occurs relatively frequently compared to any one grammatical or lexical feature, so pronunciation features are much easier to study than dialectal ones. If I were to do this project again, I would record more material in order to maximise the opportunity for the occurrence of dialectal features. Then I would edit the tape to include those features I wanted to study. In addition, I could construct a discussion which might elicit those dialectal features that I thought were important.

This study has also taught me that it is not always easy to decide whether a feature is dialectal. Several features in my transcription which looked dialectal could have been newer colloquial Standard English forms. The dividing line is often a very fine one.

Despite the depressing tone of this evaluation so far, all was not lost. I did find some grammatical and lexical features in the speech of my informant which were dialectal, but most of all, I discovered the massive differences in pronunciation between my informant's accent and RP. My informant seemed to have fewer consonants than RP, 'dropping' both /h/ and /ŋ/. He also had fewer diphthongs and short vowels than RP. He retained many of the sounds typical of older forms of English at an earlier stage in the change known as 'The Great Vowel Shift'. Indeed, his vowel system was so completely different from RP that I began to marvel that such speakers could be mutually comprehensible.

My study has certainly sharpened my ears and made me acutely aware of the sounds of the varieties of English as opposed to the spelling of English, which dominated my awareness before undertaking this project. Despite its shortcomings, the investigation has been a learning experience and was certainly worthwhile.

Exercise 1

Examples of other evaluations can be seen in the projects in Chapter 15. After studying them, read through your analysis, jotting down a brief summary of your findings and any other points of evaluation that occur to you as you go. Remember that this section should not be just a repetition in summary form of your analysis but an evaluation of the strengths and weaknesses of your work. Remember also to compare your findings with your aims in the introduction. Write up your comments so that you have a few paragraphs for your evaluation.

14

Checking and finalising

Before producing the final polished version of your project, you need to add the finishing touches, one of which is completing the bibliography (the list of all of the works that you have used to give you ideas or that you have mentioned in your project). These should be listed in alphabetical order of authors' names and laid out as suggested in Chapter 8.

You may also have additional information that you need to include. This should be put in an appendix or appendices at the end of your project. If, for instance, you have detailed tables of figures which give further support to your comments but which complicate the body of your project, then these could be placed in appendices at the back of your project. Many students, however, have no need of appendices.

Before beginning the final write-up, you need to check that you are within the word limit, if your examination board gives one. Sometimes it is difficult to keep within the word limit if your material is densely packed with significant features and you cannot omit any of the discussion. However, you should try to abide by the word limit by reorganising sections or adopting a more economical way of expressing yourself, if you possibly can. Otherwise you may find yourself penalised for excessive length. Conversely, if you are well under the word limit, then it is likely that you have not analysed your material in enough depth.

After writing up your project, check your work thoroughly. This is an important stage which many students forget about. It is also one that is not easy to do satisfactorily, as you need to view your work objectively, which is difficult to do since you actually wrote it. It is very easy to see what you *think* you have written rather than what you actually have written. You need to adopt the stance of a proof-reader and read your project through as if you have never seen it before, checking it letter by letter, word by word and for overall meaning. Check spelling in a dictionary or on a spell-checker, correct any punctuation errors, alter any awkward expression to give a more fluent style, and adjust your presentation where necessary to give a more appealing layout. The constructive, general criticism of others may be a help to you at this stage, although the proof-reading should be your own.

There is nothing wrong with a neat, handwritten project, although some people may prefer to do a typewritten project or to use a word processor. This gives them another skill in the form of keyboarding and also brings them more into contact with modern technology. Using a word processor has the added advantage of enabling you to redraft without having to rewrite completely your first versions. If you do not handwrite your project, you should try to type it yourself, so that you can say that the project is all your own work. However, remember that examiners are more impressed by content, accuracy and neatness rather than by whether a project is handwritten or typewritten.

Use wide-lined A4 paper with a margin for handwritten projects. Narrow-lined paper is more suitable for mathematical calculations and makes handwriting look squashed. If you are typing, plain white paper should be used and the lines should be double spaced. In handwritten projects, plain paper can be used for maps or any other charts which are necessary. It can also be used for the body of the project, provided that you can keep your lines straight.

Blue or black ink is required for the bulk of the writing, although you may need to use colour for clarity in parts of your transcription (see page 50) or for some charts. You should know by now which sort of pen suits you. Cheap ballpoint pens can smudge and may spoil your writing. Roller balls or fountain pens may be a better alternative. It is a good idea to put your name at the very top right-hand corner of each page of writing in case any pages become detached.

Having a dividing page with a title on it for each section makes the work look attractive. You will probably need to number each section and subsection. This is especially important in facilitating cross-referencing. There are various possibilities:

A B C D 1 2 3 4 5 6 E
1 2 3 a b 4 a b c d 5
I II (i) (ii) III IV (i) (ii) (iii) (iv) (v) V
1 2 3 4 4.1 4.2 4.3 4.3.1 4.3.2 5

You should choose a method of numbering which suits your project.

After you have written your project and numbered the pages, you should draw up a page called the contents list – this contains the main headings and subheadings with corresponding page numbers. A title page with your name, project title, examination title, candidate and centre number, if known, puts the final touch. Some students like to decorate the front page to give some colour and to convey the flavour of the project. The most important point, however, is that the content of your project is good and that it is neatly presented. The pages should be held together in some way. However, they should not be so tight as to prevent the project from being opened and the pages turned with ease. Treasury tags are a good idea for holding it together.

Exercise 1

Give your project a final check, breathe a sigh of relief and hand it in on time.

15

Completed projects

Three successful projects, two based on spoken data and one on written material, are included here as examples of the finished product. (The cover, title page and candidate's name have been omitted.) The projects are not without faults. The first project, *Airspeak*, is rather long for the word limit for some examination boards. However, it treats each of the main levels of language and it will give you some idea of the sorts of things that you can include in your own analysis.

You should not worry if you feel that your project will not reach the same standard as those included here. They are examples of what can be achieved at A level. You could still reach a high level of attainment and yet not achieve the same technical competence as in these completed projects.

Airspeak

Contents

I Introduction

English is an important medium as a lingua franca over the airwaves. However, the language of air traffic control or Airspeak has not been written about linguistically in any detail, yet there seem to be many interesting language features involved. I intend to examine the following aspects: pronunciation, vocabulary, grammar and dialogue features.

I chose Airspeak initially as I am a keen plane spotter and hope to become an air traffic controller. However, an analysis of Airspeak is also important as several 'near misses' and crashes have been blamed on unclear language use. At the end of my project, I hope to outline recommendations about language use to reduce the possibilities of misunderstandings.

II Description

The extract on the tape lasts 4 minutes and 55 seconds and was recorded in the summer of 1987. It has been edited slightly to avoid excessive silences. The extract was recorded using an airband radio on frequency 131.05 MHz which is used by the London Air Traffic Control Centre (LATCC) situated at West Drayton, just south of Heathrow Airport.

The LATCC controls all aircraft within the bounds of the London Flight Information Region (FIR) which covers England and Wales (Figure 1) and has a dense concentration of airways. The FIRs are divided into smaller sectors. The frequency 131.05 MHz controls the area known as the Pole Hill sector (Figure 2). Three reporting beacons, Pole Hill, Ottringham and Brookman's Park, are mentioned in the transcription. Inverness refers to Inverness Airport and LBA stands for the Leeds Bradford Airport.

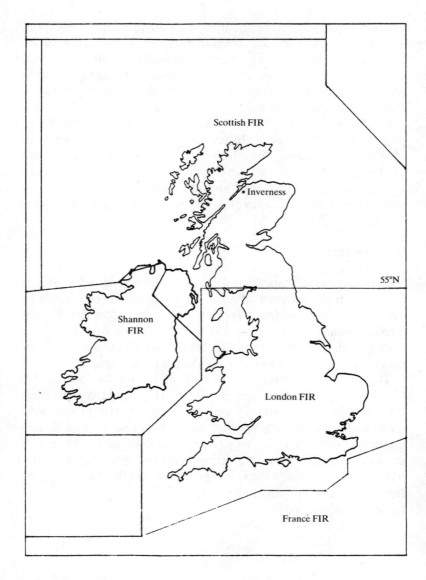

Figure 1   *Diagram to show the extent of the London Flight Information Region*

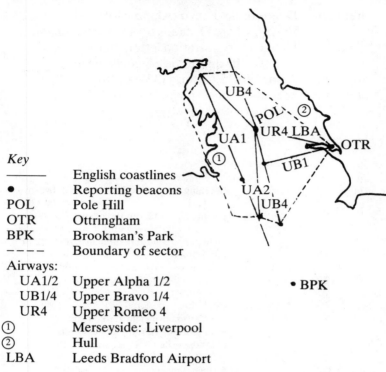

Key

———	English coastlines
•	Reporting beacons
POL	Pole Hill
OTR	Ottringham
BPK	Brookman's Park
– – – –	Boundary of sector

Airways:

UA1/2	Upper Alpha 1/2
UB1/4	Upper Bravo 1/4
UR4	Upper Romeo 4
①	Merseyside: Liverpool
②	Hull
LBA	Leeds Bradford Airport

Figure 2 *Diagram showing the extent of the Pole Hill sector*

III Transcription

(.)	– micropause
(1.0)	– timed pause
/ /	– IPA used for selected numbers only
'fast'	– prosodics used in selected places only
ATC	– air traffic controller
Station	– place of origin of radio message
Station A	– British Midland 052
Station B	– Air Canada 580
Station C	– Dan Air 152
Station D	– British Midland 344
Station E	– Beetours 17 Bravo

Station F – Delta–India–Bravo–Alpha–Hotel (D-
    IBAH, where D stands for Deutschland and
    IBAH are registration letters; the call-sign
    suggests the aircraft is privately owned)
Station G – Trans World Airlines (TWA) 761
Station H – Speedbird 283 (Speedbird is the call-sign
    used by British Airways)

Tape no.	Line no.	Speaker	
078	1	Station A	'morning London Midland (.) zero five two
			/zirəʊ faɪv tu:/
	2	'fast'	passing (.) two seven three climbing two
			/tu: sevən θri:/ /tu:
	3		eight zero requesting three five zero (2.0)'
			eɪt zirəʊ/ /θri: faɪv zirəʊ/
	4	ATC	Midland er zero five two er (.) good
	5		morning climb to flight level three
	6		one zero (.)
	7	Station A	climb three one zero (3.0)
	8	ATC	Air Canada five eight zero on your
	9		er twelve o'clock range about er ten
083	10		miles opposite direction is traffic at
	11		three five zero I'll be giving you
	12		further climb as soon as it's past (.)
	13	Station B	Air Canada thanks (9.0)
	14	Station A	Midland (.) five two is approaching three
	15		one zero (.)
	16	ATC	five two maintain three one zero on
	17		reaching (.)
	18	Station A	roger will that be cruise (.)
	19	ATC	no sir I'll give you further climb
089	20		shortly (.)
	21	Station A	okay sir (.)
	22	Station C	Dan Air one five two maintaining three
			/wɒn/
	23		one zero (2.5)
			/wɒn/
	24	ATC	Dan Air one five two thank you maintain (1.0)
			/wɒn/
	25	ATC	er Air Canada five eight zero understand
	26		there's an air traffic restriction at
	27		Brookman's Park on your clearance maintain
	28		flight level three three zero now (.)
	29	Station B	roger three three zero that's fine with
094	30		us thanks anyway thank you (.)

Tape no.	Line no.	Speaker	
	31	ATC	okay (1.0)
	32		Midland zero five two expect a higher
	33		level in about er fifteen miles (.)
	34	Station A	five two thanks (5.0)
	35	ATC	Air Canada five eight zero contact
	36		London one three four decimal seven
			/fɔ:/
	37		five good day (1.0)
	38	Station B	thirty four seventy five so long (5.0)
	39	ATC	Dan Air one five two er from your
100	40		present position you can route direct
	41		to Inverness (.)
	42	Station C	'direct Inverness one five two thanks
	43	'fast'	very much (5.0)'
	44	ATC	Midland zero one er (1.0) zero five
	45		two in your er (.) twelve o'clock range
	46		about ten miles opposite direction is
	47		traffic at three three zero as soon
	48		as it's past I'll give you further
	49		climb (.)
105	50	Station A	five two roger looking (2.0) contact five
	51		two (.)
	52	ATC	okay (10.0)
	53	Station A	roger (.) traffic's clearing down the port
	54		side (1.0)
	55	ATC	thank you Midland zero five two
	56		and er (.) climb to flight level
	57		three five zero (.)
	58	Station A	Trans Canada's DC eight yeah (1.0)
	59	ATC	that's it sir (.)
111	60	Station A	up to three five zero we're leaving
	61		three one zero (1.0)
	62	Station D	London good afternoon Midland (.) three
	63		four four level one eight zero just
			/fɔ: fɔ:/
	64		turning (.) to route direct Pole Hill (.)
	65	ATC	Midland three (.) four four good
			/fɔ: fɔ:/
	66		afternoon maintain (that?) (.)
	67	Station D	three four four (1.0)
	68	Station E	er London good afternoon Beetours
	69		one seven Bravo f. three five zero
116	70		request descent (.)
	71	ATC	er (.) Beetours one seven Bravo good
	72		afternoon er (.) maintain (.) present heading (.)
	73		and er (.) descend to flight level
	74		three (.) one zero initially please (.)
			/wʌn/

Tape no.	Line no.	Speaker	
	75	Station E	er we're heading north and we're
	76		recleared to three one zero leaving
	77		three five one seven Bravo (5.0)
	78	Station F	London Control Delta India Bravo Alpha
	79		Hotel (.) good afternoon (.)
122	80	ATC	Alpha Hotel good afternoon er
	81		direct to (.) Ottringham (.) climb to flight
	82		level two three zero please (.)
	83	Station F	er recleared two tree zero and
			/triː/
	84		up to direct Ottringham Alpha Hotel (.)
	85		roger thank you (.)
	86	Station G	London Control TWA seven six one
	87		is leaving flight level one eight (.) zero
	88		for two eight (.) zero (.)
	89	ATC	TWA seven sixty one er good afternoon
127	90		report passing flight level two seven zero please (.)
	91	Station G	'port leaving two seven zero
	92		TWA seven sixty one (1.0)
	93	ATC	Speedbird two eighty three er direct
	94		to Pole Hill (3.0)
	95	Station H	two eighty three direct to Pole Hill
	96		thank you (.)
	97	ATC	Delta (.) Alpha Hotel squawk six zero
	98		zero one please (.)
	99	Station F	six (.) zero zero one is coming down
132	100		sir (.) Alpha Hotel roger (.)
	101	ATC	thank you and call London one three
	102		four two five good day (.)
	103	Station F	one three four two five good bye to
	104		you sir (2.0)
	105	ATC	Beetours one er (.) seven Bravo er (.)
	106		route direct to er the LBA now
	107		please (.)
	108	Station E	go direct to the (.) LBAs one
	109		seven Bravo (3.0)
137	110	ATC	er Beetours one seven Bravo continue
	111		that descent to flight level (.) one (.)
	112		niner zero report approaching for
			/naɪnə/
	113		further please (.)
	114	Station E	'k recleared one nine zero call
			/naɪn/
	115		you one seven Bravo (3.0)
	116	ATC	Speedbird two eighty three London er (.)
	117		can you take flight level

Tape no.	Line no.	Speaker	
	118		three three zero (1.0)
	119	Station E	ah (.) standby one I don't think so
142	120		er (.) initially (1.0) we're looking for three
	121		one zero initially on the Atlantic clearance (3.0)
	122	ATC	er (.) roger in that case (.) er Speedbird
	123		two eighty three er (.) climb to two nine /naɪn/
	124		zero and er (.) maintain (.)
	125	Station E	roger recleared two nine zero Speedbird /naɪn/
146	126		two eight three (.)

Total time: 4 minutes 55 seconds (see CR10)

IV Analysis

A. Pronunciation

All except one of the speakers are native English speakers. Even so, there is a variety of accents ranging from British to Canadian to American English. This should not cause too many problems provided that the speech is reasonably slow. The pilots, in particular, however, speak quickly on some occasions (see lines 1–3, 42–3) and misunderstandings could occur especially if more non-native pilots were involved.

Airspeak is international and also suffers from channel limitation caused by lack of face-to-face contact and interference over the airwaves. There is therefore a special convention for the pronunciation of numbers and letters, which are extremely important in this variety. To make words carry more clearly over the airwaves, each letter is represented by a word beginning with that particular letter and each number has a specific spelling and pronunciation:

Number	Spelling	Pronunciation
0	zero	/zirəʊ/
1	wun	/wʌn/
2	too	/tu:/
3	tree	/tri:/
4	fower	/faʊə/

5	fife	/faɪf/
6	six	/sɪks/
7	seven	/seven/
8	ait	/eɪt/
9	niner	/naɪnə/

| *Spelling of word* | | *Pronunciation* |
| | decimal | /deɪsiːmæl/ |

Letter	*ATC phonetic alphabet*	*Pronunciation*
A	Alpha	/ælfæ/
B	Bravo	/brɑːvəʊ/
D	Delta	/deltæ/
H	Hotel	/həʊtel/
I	India	/ɪndiːæ/

Nine and *five* are easily confused over radio airwaves, so an extra syllable has been placed on *nine* (see line 112) and the voiced /v/ in *five* has been devoiced so shortening the vowel in *five*. This helps to differentiate between them.

The spelling of *two* as *too* is presumably to show the stressed nature of the number in contrast to the unstressed preposition *to*. The problem with these homophones is discussed later.

The spelling of *ait* for *eight* is probably to prevent problems with the 'silent letters' ⟨gh⟩ which could be a problem for foreigners.

The pronunciation of numbers coincides with the pronunciation associated with several different accents: *wun* /wʌn/ is RP and Southern. The Northern form *won* /wɒn/ is not supposed to be used but does occur (lines 22–4). Conversely, *fower* /faʊə/ corresponds to a Northern not a Southern pronunciation of *four*.

The pronunciation of *three* makes it more manageable for foreign pilots who have difficulty in saying /θ/. The German pilot uses this:

Line 83:   er recleared two *tree* zero . . .

Although *zero* rather than *nought* or *nothing* is used throughout, the pronunciations suggested for other numbers are not really used. No one other than the German pilot says /tri:/ for *three* and all occurrences of *four* are /fɔ:/ not /faʊə/. The controller does use *niner* (see line 112) but it is difficult to hear /faɪf/ being used for *five*.

Having names for letters of the alphabet means that these words are a lot clearer than simply saying the actual letters, as the letters A, E, B, C, G and P, as well as many others, could be confused with one another over the airwaves. TWA, however, is a legitimate call-sign (see lines 86, 89 and 92). 'Tango–Whiskey–Alpha' does not need to be used.

The names for the letters have their roots in different countries: *Alpha* and *Delta* are Greek, and (not in the transcription) *Papa* is French, *Whiskey* is Gaelic and *Uniform* was originally a Spanish/Portuguese word. Although English is the language of the airways, such touches give Airspeak a more international flavour.

As with numbers, some laxity in rules of pronunciation for letters appears in the extract. Stressing the vowels of normally unstressed syllables such as in *Alpha* /ælfǽ/, *Delta* /deltǽ/ and *India* /ɪndi:ǽ/ seems rare.

Pronunciation is obviously difficult to change, especially for native speakers who are expected to adopt a localised or non-native pronunciation. However, some tightening up on the pronunciation of Airspeak needs to be undertaken and pilots, in particular, should slow down the speed of their speech for the sake of clarity.

B. *Vocabulary*
Airspeak vocabulary may prove to be largely meaningless to the average lay person. Sometimes the words have a different meaning in Airspeak. Certain words are only heard in this form of English.

1. *Climb*
Climb is used frequently and means 'ascend'. It occurs both as a verb:

Line 5:   . . . *climb* to flight level three one zero

and more unusually as a non-count noun:

> Lines 47–9:   . . . as soon as it's past I'll give you further
> *climb*

Ascend is never used, although the standard form for 'go down'
is *descend*:

> Line 73:   *descend* to flight level three one zero . . .

Occasionally, the words *up to* are used:

> Line 60:   *up to* three five zero . . .

2.   Compass and clock words

Airspeak has times instead of compass bearings to inform a
pilot about another aircraft in the vicinity:

> Line 8:   Air Canada five eight zero on your er *twelve o'clock*
> range about er ten miles opposite direction . . .

The controller tells the pilot the other aircraft is at a position
equivalent to twelve o'clock from the pilot, that is straight
ahead. If the other plane had been on the starboard (right)
side, the controller would have said: 'on your three o'clock
position'. The system may have originated with war-time
'dog-fights', as it was a quick and easy way for the enemy
position to be indicated. If compass bearings were used, they
could be confused with headings. When referring to time, the
word *zulu* is used. Twelve o'clock would be: 'one two zero zero
zulu'. This prevents confusion with compass readings.

3.   Cruise

Cruise means the level at which a flight will fly at a comfortable
speed for the majority of its time:

> Line 18:   roger will that be *cruise*

Cruise is familiar in shipping and is now increasingly used for cars.

4. Heading

Heading refers to the compass heading on which an aircraft is flying. *Heading one zero zero* means that the aircraft is flying on a heading of 100° (that is 10° south of east). Pilots should say the headings as three figures but in line 75, the pilot says '. . . we're heading *north* . . .'. This is clear, however. Perhaps points of the compass should be adopted for headings rather than the use of yet more numbers which increases the possibility of a misunderstanding.

5. LBA

LBA is an acronym for the Leeds Bradford Airport. This type of word formation is increasingly common in modern English. LBA is one of a number of three-letter designated codes used in Airspeak (see line 106). They shorten the communication.

6. Level

Level means the same as *flight level* and refers to the height at which an aircraft is flying:

Line 5:   . . . *flight level* three one zero
Lines 32–3:   . . . expect a higher *level* in about er fifteen miles

In everyday English, it is unusual for *expect* to occur with distance and not with time. The abbreviation of *flight level* to *level* does not really cause problems, provided that one or the other is actually present.

7. London

London does not refer to London City but is the control centre at West Drayton. It is usually referred to as *London* or *London Control*:

Line 101:   . . . *London* one three four two five . . .

Inverness, however, refers to Inverness Airport (see line 41).

8. *Maintain*
Maintain is used instead of *keep* or *stay at/on* when flight levels or headings are involved:

Line 72:   *maintain* present heading
Lines 123–4:   climb to two nine zero and er *maintain*

9. *Numbers*
Some numbers have already been mentioned but there are various other figures which need some explanation. Anyone unused to Airspeak will be struck by the endless lists of numbers which are difficult for the lay person to interpret:

Lines 35–7:   . . . contact London *one three four decimal seven five* . . .

one three four decimal seven five refers to another frequency monitoring a different area within the London FIR (134.75 MHz). The pilots and controllers sometimes feel that it is not necessary to say the word *decimal* as every frequency has five figures. The use of the words *contact* or *call*, reminiscent of telephone usage, also indicates that frequency figures follow:

Line 101:   *call* London one three four two five good day

There is some danger, however, in omitting the word *decimal* and reducing the number of figures, as the Air Canada pilot does:

Line 38:   *thirty four seventy five*

This is an area of Airspeak communication which could be improved.

Numbers referring to flight levels have the final two zeros missing: *three three zero* means '33 000 feet'. These figures are important as aircraft have to be at least 1000 feet apart vertically and three miles horizontally. The 'vertical rules' are complied with in lines 8–12 and 44–9, where oncoming aircraft are at flight levels 35 000 and 33 000, and 33 000 and 31 000 respectively.

10. *Polite words*

A degree of politeness is apparent throughout. Pilots commonly address the controller as *sir*. Controllers do not usually address pilots as *sir*. Thus, line 59 is unusual when the controller says '. . . that's it *sir*'.

Good morning and *good afternoon* are used as greetings to indicate first contact:

Line 4:   Midland er zero five two er *good morning* . . .

Line 68:   er London *good afternoon*

Good day is used at the end of the conversation when the aircraft is leaving the sector:

Lines 101–2:   thank you and call London one three four two
                five *good day*

This could cause some confusion since Australians now tend to use *good day* to begin conversations rather than to end them. The Air Canada pilot in line 38 uses the colloquial Americanism *so long* to end the conversation.

Polite words such as *please* and *thank you* also occur quite frequently:

Line 98:   . . . squawk six zero zero one *please*

Line 30:   . . . *thanks* anyway . . .

The latter shortened colloquial form *thanks* is used by the Air Canada pilot. Generally, certain airline pilots tend to use polite terms while others don't.

11. Port and starboard

Port and *starboard*, which are also used in shipping, mean 'left' and 'right' respectively:

Line 53:   traffic's clearing down the *port* side

12. Recleared

Formations with the word *clear* are quite common. This reflects concern that flight paths are free so that aircraft can proceed without fear of collision:

Lines 26–7:   there's an air traffic restriction at Brookman's Park on your *clearance* . . .

Lines 53–4:   traffic's *clearing* down the port side

Most common is the use of the word *cleared* with the prefix *re*:

Lines 75–6:   . . . we're heading north and we're *recleared* to three one zero . . .

Line 83:   . . . *recleared* two tree zero . . .

If a pilot receives clearance to, say, a particular flight level but receives further clearance before he reaches it, this means he's been 'recleared'.

13. Report

Report is used when information is required at a later point. It means 'tell me . . .':

Line 90:   *report* passing flight level two seven zero please

14. Request

Request must be used to ask permission in Airspeak. Expressions such as *can I* could be misinterpreted:

Lines 68–70:   . . . Beetours one seven Bravo f. three five zero *request* descent

Line 3:   . . . *requesting* three five zero

15. Roger

Roger means 'I have received all your last transmission'. The pilot also often repeats the controller's message for extra clarity:

Line 29:   *roger* three three zero . . .

On occasion, the more colloquial form *okay* is used:

Line 21:   *okay* sir
Line 31:   *okay*

16. Route

Route is common in motoring but in Airspeak is usually used as a verb rather than as a noun. Conversion of this type seems to be common in Airspeak:

Lines 40–1:   . . . you can *route* direct to Inverness
Lines 63–4:   . . . just turning to *route* direct Pole Hill

17. Squawk

Squawk might normally be associated with an unpleasant bird noise but here refers to a four-digit numerical identity for each flight, which enables the aircraft to be positively identified on a controller's radar screen. In line 97, the controller instructs Delta Alpha Hotel to '*squawk* six zero zero one'. When the pilot replies, he says that the squawk is '*coming down*'. This term is used when referring to squawks because they transmit down to the ground.

18. Standby one

Standby one means 'wait one minute and I will call you':

Line 119:   *standby one* . . .

If answering was going to take longer, then the pilot may have said 'standby three' or 'standby four'.

19. Traffic
Traffic refers to vehicles on the road in everyday language. This is carried over into Airspeak where another aircraft in the vicinity is called *traffic* (see line 10).

C. Grammar
The most striking feature of Airspeak is the shortened sentences, also typical in some other forms of spontaneous spoken English, especially unscripted commentary. The omitted items are usually redundant and their inclusion would make the utterances too repetitive and long.

1. Deletion

a. Subject and predicator
Subjects and at least parts of predicators are commonly omitted giving a quick and economical method of communication like a telegram. The most common deletion is the 'empty' verb BE. Some languages do not have such a verb and usually it can be deleted with little loss to meaning. Subjects which are missing are usually pronouns, especially personal ones such as *I* or *we*, but also demonstratives such as *this*. The omitted items are usually unstressed function words. The stressed words which carry the important pieces of information are usually retained. In line 1, 'morning London Midland zero five two', the subject *this* and the predicator *is* are missing between *London* and *Midland*. In line 2, *we are* is missed out before *climbing*.

If subjects and predicators are not omitted, they are usually shortened:

Lines 120–1:   . . . *we're* looking for three one zero

This feature is typical of informal speech but is almost exclusive to native English speakers here. Foreign pilots tend to say the subject and predicator separately or else they omit them altogether:

Line 99:   six zero zero *one is* coming down

Line 83:   er recleared two tree zero . . .

One's could be used in line 99 and *we have been* has been omitted in line 83.

b. Flight level and the homophones to/two
Lines 1–3 could be rewritten fully as:

(Good) morning London (Air Traffic Control Centre). (This is British) Midland (flight number) zero five two. (We are) passing (flight level) two seven three. (We are) climbing (to flight level) two eight zero. (We are) requesting (flight level) three five zero.

The omission of *good*, the adjective pre-modifying *morning*, is a common feature in colloquial speech and does not really cause a problem in Airspeak. However, deletion of the lexical words *flight number* and *flight level* and of the preposition *to*, although this last word is a function word, can cause problems. The difficulty with *to* is mainly because it has a lexical homophone *two* which is important in Airspeak.

The omission of *flight level* and *to* has led to several fatal accidents. The recent air-miss over Clacton was caused when an American pilot mistook *two* for *to*. In 1974, a fatal accident at Gatwick Airport was caused when the pilot of an Indonesian aircraft, while trying to land in thick fog, mistook *to* for *two*, descended too far and crashed into the ground. Obviously, clarity is especially important when pilots are not native English speakers.

Between lines 1 and 3, Station A leaves out *flight level* three times, while in lines 2 and 3, because *flight level* has been omitted, it is not clear whether Station A is climbing to flight level two eight zero or climbing to flight level eight zero: 'climbing *two/to* eight zero'.

Usually, controllers use 'correct' Airspeak grammar:

> Lines 4–6: ... good morning climb *to flight level* three one zero
>
> Lines 73–4: descend *to flight level* three one zero ...

However, omission of *flight level* by the controller in line 16: 'five two maintain (flight level) three one zero' means that the numbers could have been mistaken for a heading. A further omission in line 123 is not as serious, as the preposition *to* occurs with the number *two*: 'climb *to two* nine zero'.

Other prepositions such as *at* are also omitted and this could cause confusion with the flight number:

> Lines 68–70: ... Beetours one seven Bravo (at) three five zero request descent

c. *Other deletions*

A further deletion occurs with numbers as in line 16 where the controller drops the *zero* from *Midland zero five two*. *Five two* and *zero five two* mean the same thing but the omission of numbers is a cause for concern. The only occasion when a controller drops the *zero*, however, is after the pilot has referred to himself as *five two* first (see line 14).

It is obvious from this discussion that some tightening up of deletion features to prevent misunderstanding is needed in Airspeak, especially on the part of pilots.

2. *Sentence types*

Controllers use imperatives almost all of the time as commands or instructions. The advantage is that these are brief, to the point and cannot be misunderstood:

> Lines 5–6: ... *climb* to flight level three one zero
>
> Lines 93–4: ... *direct* to Pole Hill

where *direct* is used as a verb. Other imperatives include: *maintain*, *contact*, *descend* and *continue* in lines 16, 35, 73 and 110 respectively.

Apart from being wordy, the use of an interrogative as a

polite command can cause confusion, as they are used for requests for information:

Lines 116–18:   Speedbird two eighty three London er *can you* take flight level three three zero

The aircraft involved is probably too heavy to climb any further and the controller is checking this information. This could be misunderstood as a request for action as in 'Can you pass the salt?' This is probably why interrogatives are also avoided for permission and the word *request* is used instead.

In line 118, however, the controller does try to make sure that there is no confusion by stressing the second *three* in *three three zero* to make it obvious that information about the exact flight level is required. A rising intonation is probably difficult to detect over the airwaves.

The use of post-posed subjects occurs in a couple of places:

Lines 8–11:   Air Canada five eight zero on your er twelve o'clock range about er ten miles opposite direction is *traffic* at three five zero . . .

Traffic, the subject, which would normally occur at the beginning of the sentence, appears *three* lines into the sentence. There is a good reason for this, although the sentence structure does seem awkward. The controller wants to get the most important point across first (that is 'twelve o'clock range'). In the case of an emergency, this gives the pilot a few extra seconds to spot an aircraft which may be close by.

3.   *Present participles*
Present participles are also common verb forms in Airspeak. They are mostly used by the pilots, who are indicating that some action is in progress. Often, the participles are part of a progressive verb phrase, the rest of which has been deleted:

Lines 1–3:   . . . Midland zero five two *passing* two seven three *climbing* two eight zero *requesting* three five zero

More unusually, the BE part of the progressive is present:

Lines 86–7:   . . . TWA seven six one *is leaving* flight level
one eight zero . . .

D.   *Dialogue features*
This section is designed to examine the fluency and interaction
features in Airspeak.

1. *Pauses*
Pausing is non-fluent in the middle of grammatical structures or
if it fails to occur at the end of a grammatical structure. Possibly
because the exchanges in Airspeak are relatively brief, especially on the part of the pilot, and because Airspeak contains
certain set phrases, pauses tend to be used fairly fluently, which
is good:

Lines 53–4:   roger *(.)* traffic's clearing down the port side
(1.0)

However, there are some instances of non-fluent pauses:

Lines 1–3:   morning London Midland *(.)* zero five two
passing *(.)* two seven three climbing two eight
zero requesting three five zero (2.0)

This suggests that the pilot is saying good morning to London
Midland and that something called zero five two is passing.
Extra pauses after *two seven three* and after *two eight zero*
would help to break up the lists of numbers and would make it
clear which level was being passed, which level the pilot was
climbing to, and which level he was requesting permission to
climb to. Fluent pausing in lines 1–3 might look like this:

morning London (.) Midland zero five two (.) passing two
seven three (.) climbing two eight zero (.) requesting three
five zero (2.0)

However, it might also be necessary to emphasise the important figures by pausing before them as the pilot in lines 1–3 actually does.

Another example of non-fluency occurs when the controller says a lot in one breath:

Lines 8–12:   Air Canada five eight zero on your er twelve o'clock range about er ten miles opposite direction is traffic at three five zero I'll be giving you further climb as soon as it's past

Sometimes, however, what looks like a non-fluent pause when read out is used for a good purpose:

Lines 73–4:   descend to flight level three *(.)* one zero initially please (.)

The controller here pauses after *three* to emphasise that the level is *three* and not *two*.

Long silences, which are not typical of everyday dialogue, occur during and between speakers' turns:

Lines 50–1:   five two roger looking *(2.0)* contact five two

The 2 second pause is because the pilot needs time to act upon instructions. He stops to look for another plane. Controllers do not give out continuous commands to the same pilot, since he may not have had enough time to carry out the first order before receiving another.

2. *Pause fillers*

Pause fillers are also rare in Airspeak. The hesitation *er*, however, does occur as an utterance initiator both for the controller and for the pilots:

Lines 25–7:   *er* Air Canada five eight zero understand there's an air traffic restriction at Brookman's Park . . .

Line 75:   *er* we're heading north . . .

Er in the middle of utterances, however, occurs wholly on the part of the controller. This is probably because pilots say relatively little, and know where they are and what they intend to do. Controllers have to think about what has happened and about what commands they will give out next:

Lines 4–5:   Midland *er* zero five two *er* (.) good morning . . .

Lines 8–10:   Air Canada five eight zero on your *er* twelve o'clock range about *er* ten miles . . .

Lines 55–7:   thank you Midland zero five two and *er* (.) climb to flight level three five zero

3.   Self-correction

On one occasion, the controller makes a mistake:

Lines 44–5:   Midland zero one *er (1.0)* zero five two

This could be seen as referring to 'flight zero one zero five two' and not 'flight zero five two'. The controller here has gone against a rule about using the word *correction*. He should have said: 'Midland zero one er *correction* zero five two' to avoid any chance of confusion.

4.   Turn-taking

An unusual dialogue feature of Airspeak is the repetition of what a speaker has said in a previous turn:

Lines 5–7 ATC: . . . climb to flight level three one zero
        Station A: *climb three one zero*

Lines 27–9 ATC: . . . maintain flight level three three zero now
        Station B: roger *three three zero* . . .

This procedure is adopted so that the pilot can confirm the controller's instructions. It gives the controller an opportunity to check that he has given the correct message and to correct any misunderstanding on the pilot's part.

A feature common in spontaneous dialogue but totally

absent here is overlapping. The turn-taking is orderly. Simultaneous speech would obviously cause problems of misunderstanding.

A further unusual dialogue feature is that the controller is carrying on several separate conversations at the same time. Between lines 65 and 72, the controller greets and gives instructions to Station D, answers Station E's greeting and gives instructions to him as well. Between line 72 and the end of the transcription, the controller speaks to a further three pilots and still maintains contact with Station E. This is a potential area for confusion, as the number of aircraft that a controller can handle at any one time is limited only by the ruling about the distances that aircraft have to be apart.

V Evaluation

In this project, I have shown how Airspeak:

1 has adopted an unusual pronunciation for numbers and letters;
2 has specific and unusual vocabulary, sometimes associated with other modes of transport or with other means of communication through the airwaves, occasionally involving conversion and the use of acronyms;
3 uses specific sentence types involving deletion, imperatives, present participles and post-position;
4 has few non-fluency features, an orderly but unusual pattern of turn-taking with frequent silences, common repetition of a previous speaker's words, and several 'conversations' being carried on at once.

After analysing the transcription, several communication problems have become apparent. These could be remedied as follows:

1 The pronunciation rules for numbers and letters should always be adhered to, although there are occasions, as with headings, when numbers could be replaced by other words,

which might aid communication.

2   Care must be taken with deletion, especially with lexical items such as the company name or *flight level*, and with prepositions such as *to*, otherwise it is not always clear which blocks of numbers refer to flight number, flight level, heading and so on.

3   Self-corrections should always be prefaced with the word *correction* and pauses should be used more judiciously, if possible, to aid communication. Pilots could speak more slowly and a limit should be placed on the number of aircraft a controller deals with at any one time, to prevent him from handling too many conversations at once.

4   Good practices such as the use of direct imperatives, the post-posing of less important information, the repetition of the previous speaker's words and orderly, polite turn-taking should be reinforced.

I feel that my project has been a very worthwhile undertaking as I have described the main features of a little researched but increasingly important variety of English. In addition, if my recommendations were adopted, I feel that accidents and air-misses might be reduced.

VI   Bibliography

Background reading
Civil Aviation Authority 'Britain's Civil Aviation Authority' Document no. 225 London: CAA
Civil Aviation Authority 'National Air Traffic Services' (1987) Document no. 257 London: CAA
Duke, Graham (1987) *Aircraft Illustrated Special* 'Air Traffic Control' London: Ian Allen Ltd
Howells, H. and Worrall, G. (1983) *Aircraft Radios and Airways* Manchester: Cheshire Aviation Society

The language of some students with learning difficulties and their teacher

Contents

I Introduction

The area that I have chosen to study for my project is the speech of some students with learning difficulties and the language their teacher uses to encourage them to converse. I hope to concentrate on features typical of teacher talk and of adult usage to young children. This includes: questioning, prosodics, repetition and expansion, the control of turn-taking, the use of encouraging words and sounds, and the avoidance of pronouns on the part of the teacher. For the students, some mention will be made of their pronunciation, vocabulary, grammar and turn-taking patterns.

II Description

The material used is a recorded extract from a lesson consisting of five students, who are often called mentally handicapped in everyday usage, and their teacher. The students involved are: Jamie, Desmond, Thomas, Shaun and Stephen. They range from 17 to 19 years of age but have been adjudged to have mental ages of around four to seven years.

All the students attend Castledon Special School and live in and around Garmouth. Most of them have attended this school from the age of six or seven years. When the recording was made, the class was involved in a discussion referred to as 'conversational therapy' by their teacher. In the transcription, the teacher discusses the colour of some items of their clothing and their outing earlier that day to the swimming baths.

The students learn to appreciate and become firm friends with their teacher. However, if a stranger enters the room, they become very distracted. Some will immediately become quiet and unresponsive, while others will be very inquisitive and loudly question the intruder. To record 'natural' speaking and conversational features with the teacher, it was necessary to use a hidden microphone, known only to the teacher.

III Transcription

Key
(.)　– micropause
(1.0)　– timed pause
ˇ ˆ　– tones on selected items only
"　– contrastive stress on selected syllables
/wed/ – phonetic symbols for selected words (/w/ = labialised
　　/r/)
=　– latching on
∥ ∥　– overlapping
[ ]　– background noise or unclear speech

Tape no.	Line no.	Speaker	
148	1	Teacher	rîght (2.0) and what's Mr Puckering
	2		wéaring
	3	Jamie	(4.0) shirt (2.0)
	4	Teacher	"blue shirt (.)
	5	Jamie	blue sh (.)
	6	Teacher	[and] what's Desmond wéaring
	7	Desmond	(3.0) errh =
	8	Teacher	= who's this
	9	Desmond	(.) Jamie (.)
153	10	Teacher	what's Desmond wearing
	11	Jamie	(3.5) er um
	12	Shaun	[laugh snort]
	13	Unknown	who was that (.)
	14	Teacher	who's (.) what's Desmond wearing
	15	Jamie	(1.0) blue (.)
	16	Teacher	blue what
	17	Jamie	(2.0) blue (1.0)
	18	Teacher	blue júmper (.)
	19	Jamie	jumper (.) /bʒəmpə/
158	20	Teacher	no it's (2.0) not really blue is it (.) [background noise incomprehensible]
	21	Shaun	he says it's a grey jumper =
	22	Teacher	= what (.)
	23		what colour jumper (.)
	24	Shaun	red and = /wed n̩/
	25	Desmond	= grey (.) /greːə/
	26	Teacher	"grey jumper (.)
	27	Jamie	grey (.) /grɛə/

Tape no.	Line no.	Speaker	
	28	Teacher	that's right =
	29	Shaun	= grey
			/greə/
161	30	Shaun	and it's got (.) what is it (2.0) red (.)
	31	Teacher	and what colour jumper has Jamie got on
	32	Desmond	(1.0) blue (.)
	33	Jamie	blue (.)
	34	Teacher	blue jumper (.) yes (.)
	35	Shaun	like (.) you
	36	Shaun	// um //
	37	Teacher	// m //
	38		[incomprehensible] Desmond are you
			/e:pɒnsæ/
	39		going to tell us a story (.)
165	40		what have you done this morning
	41	Desmond	(3.0) been (.) outside (.) cn (4.0) swimming
	42	Teacher	hm. hm (1.0) and who were you
	43		swimming with
	44	Desmond	(1.0) Judith (.)
	45	Teacher	mhm =
	46	Desmond	= and you (.) and (4.0) all of (.) the
	47		class (.)
	48	Teacher	mm (.) did you enjoy swimming (.)
	49	Desmond	yes (.)
171	50	Teacher	mm (3.0) did Jamie swim (.)
	51	Jamie	yeah (.)
	52	Teacher	what did Jamie do (.)
	53	Jamie	// Jamie // (.)
	54	Shaun	// [anything really] //
	55	Teacher	did you make a big splash (.)
	56	Desmond	// huh nothing //
	57	Jamie	// yeah // (.)
	58	Teacher	did you (2.0) did you go under the
	59		water
174	60	Jamie	(1.0) yes (3.5)
	61	Unknown	[the plug's in there] (3.0)
	62	Teacher	Thomas what did you do (2.5) did Thomas
	63		swim
	64	Thomas	(6.0) yeah // [I did] //
	65	Teacher	// what // about Stephen
	66	Stephen	(3.0) we done lessons about (2.0)
	67	Desmond	djum =
	68	Stephen	= how
	69		to get gra. (1.0) grade badges (.)
179	70	Desmond	mhmm
	71	Stephen	(3.0) like mushroom floats (2.0)
			/floəts/
	72	Teacher	mhm (2.5)
	73	Stephen	and lying on your back (.)
	74	Teacher	Shaun how did you get to the baths
	75	Shaun	(2.0) by the coach (.)
	76	Teacher	mhmm (.)

Tape no.	Line no.	Speaker	
	77	Shaun	we took all of the swimming gear
	78		(2.5) and we took all the swimming boards (.)
			/bɔːədz/
	79	Teacher	mhm (.)
186	80	Shaun	'nd we took (2.0) and we got ready (1.5)
			/wedi:/
	81		in the changing rooms (.)
	82	Teacher	and did you all jump in the water
	83	Shaun	(1.0) yeah (.)
	84	Stephen	I did (.)
	85	Teacher	there was one boy who didn't jump
	86		in the water (.)
	87	Stephen	Shaun Galilee (.)
	88	Teacher	who was it
	89		Thomas (.)
190	90	Thomas	Tom Ganinee (.)
			/tom gænɪni:/
	91	Teacher	[and] what did Shaun do
	92	Thomas	(1.0) sat on the s. (1.0) step (.)
	93	Teacher	sat on the steps (.) and wouldn't he go
	94		in (.)
	95	Shaun	[laugh]
	96	Thomas	well (.) did a splash (.)
	97	Teacher	he did a splash with his legs (.) can
	98		you learn to swim by splashing with
	99		your legs (2.5) I think you've got
194	100		to get in the water haven't you (1.0)
	101		if // you're // going to swim (.)
	102	Unknown	yeah yeah (.)
	103	Teacher	who tried hard at swimming (.)
	104	Stephen	me (.)
	105	Desmond	and me (.)
	106	Teacher	what did you do Desmond (1.0) you're
	107		going to try hard at swimming (.) you tell (.)
	108	Desmond	err [whisper] I can learn how to
	109		swim on me back n (.) on me (.) front
			/frʊn/
	110		(2.0) and er (2.0) down

(see CR11)

IV   Analysis

A.   Teacher's language

1.   Questioning

Of the 37 turns which the teacher has, 27 are questions and 18 of these are *wh*-questions. It is clear that there would have been very little dialogue at all if the teacher hadn't been there and that a major way of drawing out conversation from the students is by means of a question–answer technique. The teacher uses *wh*-questions mainly because these are more open ended than *yes–no* questions:

Line 40:   *what* have you done this morning

Line 74:   Shaun *how* did you get to the baths

Often, these questions have to be repeated before an answer is forthcoming:

Line 6:   [and] *what's* Desmond wearing

Line 10:   *what's* Desmond wearing

Line 14:   who's (.) *what's* Desmond wearing

This illustrates the great patience needed by the teacher to obtain an answer from the less able students.

Sometimes a question is asked after it has already been answered:

Line 85   Teacher: there was one boy who didn't jump
    86   in the water (.)
    87   Stephen: Shaun Galilee (.)
    88   Teacher: *who was it*
    89   Thomas (.)
    90   **Thomas:**   Tom Ganinee (.)

This is to give the less able students a chance to answer a question to which they have already heard the answer. Many have difficulty in retaining information for any length of time.

Sometimes the *wh*-word used by the teacher provides a 'space' to be filled in by the student:

Line 16:   blue *what*

Sometimes *yes–no* questions are used. This is mainly with the less able students who cannot manage much more than one-word answers:

Line 50   Teacher: mm (3.0) *did* Jamie swim (.)
    51   Jamie: yeah (.)

Occasionally, these *yes–no* questions are tags which require feedback in the form of agreement:

Lines 99–101:   ... I think you've got to get in the water
                haven't you (1.0) if you're going to swim
Line 20:   ... it's (2.0) not really blue *is it*

The tag in line 20 gently points out that the student was wrong in his first assumption about colour.

The question–answer technique which employs questions to which answers are already known is typical not only of teacher talk but, as pointed out by Freeborn (1986: 122), occurs in a mother's use to a child, as the child learns the social rules of turn-taking.

2.   *Prosodics*

Another technique common in 'caretaker speech' is the exaggerated use of intonation:

Line 1:   *rîght* (2.0) and what's Mr Puckering
    2:   *wéaring*

Here, the rise-fall on *right* produces encouragement for the student to answer. The rise at the end of the question, more common in *yes–no* questions, emphasises that the utterance is a question and needs to be answered.

Contrastive stress is also employed to highlight particular words:

Line 4:   *"blue* shirt
Line 26:   *"grey* jumper

The teacher has strongly stressed a word which under normal conversational circumstances would not be greatly stressed. This is to emphasise vocabulary 'new' to the student and to encourage the student to produce these words.

3. Repetition and expansion

Again, as in child language acquisition situations, the teacher represents a correct model of language that the students here can copy. Sometimes the teacher repeats and expands on what the student has initially said. The student can then try to reiterate what the teacher has said:

Line 3	Jamie:	shirt (2.0)
4	Teacher:	"blue shirt (.)
5	Jamie:	blue sh (.)
Line 15	Jamie:	(1.0) blue (.)
16	Teacher:	blue what
17	Jamie:	(2.0) blue (1.0)
18	Teacher:	blue jumper (.)
19	Jamie:	jumper (.)
Line 96	Thomas:	well (.) did a splash (.)
97	Teacher:	he did a splash with his legs . . .

In line 97, the teacher has expanded the student's version by adding a subject, the pronoun *he*, and an adverbial *with his legs*.

Line 91	Teacher:	[and] what did Shaun do
92	Thomas:	(1.0) sat on the s. (1.0) step (.)
93	Teacher:	sat on the steps . . .

In line 93, the teacher has not overtly corrected Thomas but has produced the correct version immediately after Thomas's version to reinforce what it should be.

4. Control of turn-taking

The teacher obviously dominates the conversation and has to control turn-taking in order to 'provoke' conversation 'evenly' from all students, so that they all have a chance of improving their speech:

Line	6	Teacher:	[and] what's Desmond wearing
	7	Desmond:	(3.0) errh =
	8	Teacher:	= *who's this*
	9	Desmond:	(.) Jamie (.)
	10	Teacher:	what's Desmond wearing
	11	Jamie:	(3.5) er um

Here, the original question in line 6 was aimed at Jamie. However, when he fails to answer, Desmond begins to speak. The teacher interjects before Desmond is able to give the answer and asks a very simple question (line 8) that brings the question back round to Jamie (line 9). The teacher then repeats the original question (line 10) and is successful in obtaining at least an utterance from Jamie.

The teacher also ensures an equal share in the conversation by directly naming the student who is to answer. This also attracts the attention of the particular student, as the vocative usually occurs at the beginning of the sentence before the question:

Line 62: *Thomas* what did you do (2.5) . . .

Between lines 1 and 37, the teacher has concentrated on Jamie. In line 38, he switches his attention to Desmond:

Lines 38–9: *Desmond* are you going to tell us a story (.) . . .

After speaking briefly to Thomas in line 62, he then addresses Stephen and finally Shaun:

Line 65: what about *Stephen*

Line 74: *Shaun* how did you get to the baths

On one occasion, when the teacher has the conversation flowing smoothly and virtually all of the students' interest, he asks a question for anyone to answer, directed at no one in particular:

Line 103:   who tried hard at swimming (.)

These undirected questions are rare, however.

It is obvious that the situation here demands great skill in controlling the conversation on the part of the teacher.

5.   *Encouraging words and sounds*

Again, as in adult usage to young children, the teacher uses phrases or expressions such as *mhm* or *hmhm* to reward the students for their responses and to encourage them to continue:

| Line 27 | Jamie: | grey (.) |
| 28 | Teacher: | *that's right* |

Line 41	Desmond:	(3.0) been (.) outside (.) cn (4.0) swimming
42	Teacher:	*hm. hm.* (1.0) and who were you
43		swimming with
44	Desmond:	(1.0) Judith (.)
45	Teacher:	*mhm* =
46	Desmond:	= and you (.)
47		and (4.0) all of (.) the class (.)

6.   *Avoidance of pronouns*

Pronouns are often one of the last grammatical features that young children completely master. This is not only because they 'stand for' another noun, but because their reference varies according to who the speaker or hearer is. For instance, the teacher could address any of the students as *you* but they would refer to themselves as *I* and the teacher as *you*. In several places here, the teacher both controls the turns by naming the speaker in the third person and avoids the complexity inherent in the more normal second person pronoun of direct address, *you*:

Line 50	Teacher:	mm (3.0) did *Jamie* swim (.)
51	Jamie:	yeah (.)
Line 62	Teacher:	Thomas what did you do (2.5) did *Thomas*
63		swim

B.   Students' language

1.   Pronunciation

In some of the literature I read, the term 'mental retardation' was used to denote a 'slowing down' in the process involved in learning. It is no surprise therefore that the students in the transcription show language features typical of children of a much younger age. Many of the pronunciation difficulties encountered by the students are characteristic of normal children between the ages of one and a half and four years.

/r/ is one of the last sounds to be properly mastered by children, and even some adults have problems with it. A labialised version rather like the semi-vowel /w/ is often substituted for /r/. This occurs in the speech of Shaun:

> Line 24:   red and
>   /wed/
> Line 80:   'nd we took (2.0) and we got ready
>   /wedi:/

Plosives are usually acquired before fricatives, and affricates, which are a combination of both these types of consonants, are often problematic for young children. Jamie in the word *jumper* manages the fricative part of /dʒ/ but has substituted a labial plosive /b/ for the alveolar /d/ which is further back in the mouth than /b/:

> Line 19:   jumper (.)
>   /bʒəmpə/

Consonants such as /b/, which is formed at the front of the mouth, are easier to produce, so 'fronting' often occurs in the speech of young children.

The substitution of a plosive (also called a stop) for a fricative occurs in Thomas's speech when he uses the plosive /t/ for the fricative /ʃ/ when trying to say *Shaun*:

    Line 90:   Tom Ganinee (.)
                  /tɒm gænɪni:/

The word Thomas produces is very like his own name *Tom* as the final nasal /n/ has also been fronted and labialised to /m/. Thomas also has problems with /l/ in the same utterance. The /l/s in the word *Galilee* have become /n/s. The nasal /n/ is usually learnt by young children before the liquid /l/ and this probably explains Thomas's difficulty.

Another pronunciation difficulty encountered by both young, normal children and these older special needs students is when the syllable structure involves a consonant cluster:

    Line 109:   swim on me back n (.) on me front
                                       /frʊn/

Here, Desmond manages the consonant cluster at the beginning of the word *front* but not at the end. He reduces the cluster so that the word has a CCVC structure instead of a CCVCC structure. Adults, however, also sometimes elide one consonant in a cluster in continuous speech.

A number of the students in this transcription have difficulty in holding on to what in the local accent would be simple long vowels:

    Line 27   Jamie: grey (.)
                      /grɛə/

    Line 71   Stephen: (3.0) like mushroom floats (2.0)
                                /floəts/

    Line 78   Shaun: (2.5) and we took all the swimming
                             boards (.)
                             /bɔːədz/

In each case, the student has diphthongised a monophthong, /eː/, /oː/ and /ɔː/ respectively, in local speech. Again, this is similar to unstable vowel usage in young children.

2. *Vocabulary*

The vocabulary in this extract tends to be fairly simple and concrete, involving mainly items of clothing such as *shirts*, *jumpers* and *swimming gear*. *Mushroom floats* is probably a childish expression for the swimming manoeuvre which has been used by an adult so that the action can be more easily understood by the students (see line 71).

Colours, however, present some difficulty and are not easily learned by children. It is necessary to know not only which colours the words refer to, but also where the boundaries are between the different colours before colour words can be correctly used. Jamie obviously has great difficulty here and calls something *blue* which is *grey*. Shaun and Desmond are obviously more sophisticated in naming the colours of the jumper:

Line 24   Shaun: *red* and =
   25   Desmond: = *grey* (.)

3. *Grammar*

The students vary in their level of acquisition. This is shown by the degree to which they can answer questions using full sentences. Jamie, who has severe learning difficulties and has a mental age of four, can manage only one-word answers:

Line 1   Teacher: right (2.0) and what's Mr Puckering
   2   wearing
   3   Jamie: (4.0) *shirt* (2.0)

Jamie's answer in line 3 is a monosyllabic, concrete, count noun, but he has been unable to use the indefinite article *a* which is a function word. He later manages to repeat the adjective *blue* after the teacher, but is unable to complete the word *shirt*, as he has difficulty in producing two-word utterances:

Line 5:   blue *sh* (.)

Throughout the transcription, he manages only one-word utterances such as *jumper* and, apart from answering *yeah*, the other words such as *grey* or *blue* are repetitions of what someone else has said. Jamie therefore does not show much knowledge of word classes.

On one occasion, Jamie answers irrelevantly by merely repeating his name, which is familiar to him:

> Line 52   Teacher: what did Jamie do (.)
>   53   Jamie: *Jamie*

He seems to misunderstand *wh*-questions but can recognise *yes–no* questions, as he answers them with *yeah*:

> Line 50   Teacher: mm (3.0) did Jamie swim (.)
>   51   Jamie: *yeah* (.)

The kind of repetitive one-word answers produced by Jamie are usual for a child much younger than four. By four, normal children are able to create new sentences. Jamie's behaviour is generally only imitative.

In contrast to Jamie, Shaun and Stephen, who have more minor learning difficulties, can manage full sentences:

> Line 21   Shaun: he says it's a grey jumper
> Lines 77–8   Shaun: we took all of the swimming gear
>   (2.5) and we took all the swimming
>   boards (.)
> Lines 66–9   Stephen: (3.0) we done lessons about (2.0)
>   how to get gra. (1.0) grade badges
>   (.)

In line 21, Shaun manages a sentence with a whole clause as an object, while in lines 77–8, he uses the conjunction *and* as a continuer. Stephen, in line 66, uses the local dialect form *done* for the past tense of *do* rather than the Standard English form *did*. However, some childish errors still occur:

Line 74   Teacher: Shaun how did you get to the baths
  75   Shaun: (2.0) by *the* coach (.)

In line 75, Shaun has assumed that the coach is a definite known one.

Desmond, who has moderate learning difficulties, falls somewhere between Jamie, and Shaun and Stephen. He manages some sentences but they are sometimes hesitant and abbreviated:

Line 41:   (3.0) been (.) outside (.) cn (4.0) swimming

The same can be said for Thomas who omits the subject and adverbial in line 96:

Line 96   Thomas: well (.) did a splash (.)
  97   Teacher: *he* did a splash *with his legs* (.)

4. *Turn-taking*

Shaun, Stephen and Desmond behave like older children in a family who have acquired more language than their younger brothers and sisters. They are ready to answer for the students with more severe learning difficulties:

Line 31   Teacher: and what colour jumper has Jamie got
                       on
  32   Desmond: (1.0) *blue* (.)
  33   Jamie: blue (.)
Line 23   Teacher: what colour jumper (.)
  24   Shaun: *red* and =
  25   Desmond: = *grey*
                                                    (.)

The students with more severe learning difficulties have longer pauses before they begin to answer and in the middle of utterances as they take longer to think about what they are going to say:

```
Line 1   Teacher:   right (2.0) and what's Mr Puckering
     2              wearing
     3   Jamie:              (4.0) shirt (2.0)
Line 62  Teacher:   Thomas what did you do (2.5) did
    63              Thomas swim
    64   Thomas:             (6.0) yeah
```

However, fairly long pauses seem generally typical of all the students' speech:

```
Line 65  Teacher:   what about Stephen
    66   Stephen:   (3.0) we done
    67              lessons about (2.0)
    68              how
    69              to get gra. (1.0) grade badges (.)
```

Patience is obviously again required on the part of the hearer, as the speech is very slow.

V   Evaluation

My study of the language of students with special educational needs in their late teens has shown a great similarity between their language and the language of normal children of a much younger age who are just acquiring the language. Similarly, the language which the teacher uses has features in common not only with teacher talk, but also with the language that adults use to infants and very young children. Just as normal children of the same age learn language at varying rates, so the wide range of levels of ability among these students of similar ages means that they show a huge variation in the stages of language acquisition. Although the students are adjudged to have a particular mental age, for those with the most severe learning difficulties, language acquisition seems to be further behind than what would be expected of a normal child with the same chronological age. The teacher showed great skill and patience in encouraging the students and in coping with their differing degrees of progress.

The subject of language and special needs has not been covered much in the literature. I hope that I have produced an informative project that will interest and enlighten the reader about this subject.

VI Bibliography

Freeborn, D. (1986) *Varieties of English* London: Macmillan

Background reading
Lloyd, P. *et al.* (1984) *Introduction to Psychology* London: Fontana
Schiefelbusch, R.L. *et al.* (1967) *Language and Mental Retardation* New York: Holt, Rinehart and Winston

Chaucer's English

Contents

I Introduction

In this project, I hope to discover the differences between a piece of Late Middle English, written towards the end of the fourteenth century, and the same extract in Modern English. I decided to do this topic because I was fascinated by language change when I came across the Late Middle English writings of Geoffrey Chaucer in English Literature classes. The written word has allowed us to communicate through time and it intrigued me to think that I could actually work out how language was used all those centuries ago. I decided to take this opportunity of investigating the changes in spelling, vocabulary and grammar in the hope that it would improve my understanding both of that particular text and of language change in general.

II Description

The extract under study involves 36 lines from a description of a character called the Pardoner in Geoffrey Chaucer's *The General Prologue to the Canterbury Tales*. The book contains a number of detailed descriptions of contrasting medieval characters who are on their way to Canterbury on a pilgrimage. Chaucer describes each one and then allows many to tell a story on the journey. Pardoners used to sell documents from the church called pardons. These allowed people to build up credit against their sins. The extract under consideration tells of this particular Pardoner's appearance and the tricks he used to extract money from poor people. I chose it because it seemed to contain some interesting language features.

Geoffrey Chaucer is often considered to be the father of English literature, as much writing before his time was in Latin or, especially after the Norman Conquest, in French. The period from about 1100 to about 1450 or 1500 is generally known as Middle English. It differs from Old English because of French and Scandinavian influence. From around about the Renaissance onwards, further changes make the language more like Modern English. Chaucer wrote the extract under study in a South Eastern dialect of English in the Late Middle English period, some time between 1387 and 1392.

My data is presented in four ways:

1   A facsimile of the Hengwrt manuscript (Manuscript A) which I managed to obtain from the local university with the help of the local librarian. This is important for the study of the orthography.

2   A transcription of the Hengwrt manuscript in modern type with variant spellings from the Ellesmere manuscript. The Hengwrt and Ellesmere manuscripts are usually accepted as being of superior authority to most of the other 80 or so manuscripts in existence.

3   A modern version of the extract (Manuscript B), edited by James Winny, taken from the book we use in class. This is the version that most people are familiar with, but it contains a number of alterations from the original, especially in graphology.

4   My own modern translation (Manuscript C) which is useful when contrasting vocabulary and grammar with Middle English usage.

Wherever I needed to check on the relationship between spelling and pronunciation, I did this by using a library recording with a reconstructed fourteenth century pronunciation.

III   Data

1.   Manuscript A – facsimile
The following facsimile from the Hengwrt manuscript, lines 669–704, describes a character called the Pardoner in Geoffrey Chaucer's *The General Prologue to the Canterbury Tales*.

Pardoner
670

With hym ther rood a gentil pardoner
Of Rouncivale his freend and his compeer
That streight was comen fro the court of Rome
Ful loude he soong com hider love to me

675

This somonour bar to hym a stif burdoun
Was nevere trompe of half so greet a soun
This pardoner hadde heer as yelow as wex
But smothe it heeng as dooth a strike of flex
By ounces henge his lokkes þt he hadde
And ther with he his shuldres overspradde
680
But thynne it lay by colpons oon and oon
But hood for jolitee wered he noon
For it was trussed up in his walet
Hym thoughte he rood al of the newe jet
Dischevelee save his cappe he rood al bare
685
Swiche glarynge eyen hadde he as an hare
A vernycle hadde he sowed up on his cappe
His walet biforn hym in his lappe
Bretful of pardon comen from Rome al hoot
A voys he hadde as smal as hath a goot
690
No berd hadde he ne nevere sholde have
As smothe it was as it were late yshave
I trowe he were a geldyng or a mare
But of his craft fro Berwyk in to Ware
Ne was ther swich another pardoner
695
For in his male he hadde a pilwe beer
Which þt he seyde was oure lady veyl
He seyde he hadde a gobet of the seyl
That seint peter hadde whan þt he wente
Up on the see til Jhu Crist hym hente
700
He hadde a cros of latoun ful of stones
And in a glas he hadde pigges bones
But with thise relikes whan þt he foond
A poure persoun dwellyng up on lond
Up on a day he gat hym moore moneye
Than þt the persoun gat in monthes tweye

2.   *Manuscript A – transcription*

The following is a transcription of lines 669–704 of the Hengwrt manuscript with variant readings from the Ellesmere manuscript:

Pardoner ¶With hym ther rood / a gentil Pardoner
670 Of Rouncyual / his freend / and his comper
    That streight was comen / fro the Court of Rome
    Ful loude he soong7 com hyder loue to me

    This Somonour baar to hym / a styf burdoun
    Was neuere trompe / of half so greet a soun
675 ¶This Pardoner / hadde heer / as yelow as wex
    But smothe it heeng7 as dooth a stryke of flex
    By ounces / henge his lokkes þat he hadde
    And ther with / he his shuldres ouerspradde
    But thynne it lay / by colpons oon and oon
680 But hood for Iolitee / wered he noon
    For it was trussed vp / in his walet7
    Hym thoughte / he rood al of the newe Iet7
    Discheuelee saue his cappe / he rood al bare
    Swiche glarynge eyen / hadde he as an hare
685 A vernycle / hadde he sowed / vp on his cappe
    His walet7 biforn hym / in his lappe
    Bretful of pardoun / comen from Rome al hoot7
    A voys he hadde / as smal / as hath a Goot7
    No berd hadde he / ne neuere sholde haue
690 As smothe it was / as it were late yshaue
    I trowe he were a geldyng7 or a Mare
    But of his craft7. fro Berwyk in to Ware
    Ne was ther / swich another Pardoner
    For in his Male / he hadde a pilwe beer
695 Which þat he seyde / was oure lady veyl
    He seyde he hadde / a gobet of the seyl
    That Seint Peter hadde / whan þat he wente
    Vp on the See / til Iesu Crist hym hente
    He hadde a cros of latoun / ful of stones
700 And in a glas / he hadde pigges bones
    But with thise relykes / whan þat he foond
    A poure person / dwellyng vp on lond
    Vp on a day / he gat hym moore moneye
    Than þat the persoun gat7 in Monthes tweye

ELLESMERE

¶Pardoner]	With	ther was / a
Rounciuale /	freend	compeer
court		
hider		

ELLESMERE

18	Somonour / bar	hym	stif
neuere			
This Pardoner			
strike			
hise			
hise	ouerspradde		

trussed / vp
rood /

eyen
vernycle

Bret ful	hoot /
smal	goot /
neuere	
shaue	
trowe /	geldyng	mare
craft7	Berwyk,	

male,

gobet7
seint
crist
croys

| with | relikes / | fond |
| persoun / dwellynge | | lond |

person gat /

3.   *Manuscript B – modern version*

The following is a modern version of Manuscript A taken from Winny (1976: 72–3) lines 671–706:

670
        With him ther rood a gentil PARDONER
        Of Rouncivale, his freend and his compeer,
        That streight was comen fro the court of Rome.
        Ful loude he soong 'Com hider, love, to me!'
        This Somonour bar to him a stif burdoun;
        Was nevere trompe of half so greet a soun.
        This Pardoner hadde heer as yelow as wex,
        But smothe it heeng as dooth a strike of flex;
        By ounces henge his lokkes that he hadde,
680 And therwith he his shuldres overspradde;
        But thinne it lay, by colpons oon and oon.
        But hood, for jolitee, wered he noon,
        For it was trussed up in his walet.
        Him thoughte he rood al of the newe jet;
        Dischevelee, save his cappe, he rood al bare.
        Swiche glaringe eyen hadde he as an hare.
        A vernicle hadde he sowed upon his cappe.
        His walet lay biforn him in his lappe,
        Bretful of pardoun, comen from Rome al hoot.
690 A voys he hadde as smal as hath a goot.
        No berd hadde he, ne nevere sholde have;
        As smothe it was as it were late shave.
        I trowe he were a gelding or a mare.
        But of his craft, fro Berwik into Ware,
        Ne was ther swich another pardoner.
        For in his male he hadde a pilwe-beer,
        Which that he seyde was Oure Lady veil:
        He seyde he hadde a gobet of the seil
        That Seint Peter hadde, whan that he wente
700 Upon the see, til Jhesu Crist him hente.
        He hadde a crois of latoun ful of stones,
        And in a glas he hadde pigges bones.
        But with thise relikes, whan that he fond
        A povre person dwellinge upon lond,
        Upon a day he gat him moore moneye
        Than that the person gat in monthes tweye;

4. *Manuscript C – translation into Modern English*

The following is my own translation of the extract into Modern English:

671 With him, there rode a charming Pardoner
from Charing Cross, his friend and his companion,
who had come straight from the Vatican in Rome.
He sang 'Come hither, love, to me!' very loudly.
The Summoner supported him with a strong bass.
No trumpet ever made half as much noise.
The Pardoner had hair as yellow as wax
but it hung lankly like a hank of flax does.
What hair he had hung in rats-tails
680 and he covered his shoulders with it
but it lay thinly in strands here and there.
He didn't wear any hood in order to be festive
for it was packed away in his saddlebag.
    It seemed to him that he rode totally in the latest style.
Except for his skull-cap, he rode bare-headed with loose,
                                             untidy hair.
He had such staring eyes like a hare.
He had sewn a Veronica on to his cap.
His saddlebag lay in front of him on his lap,
brimful of pardons having just come hot from Rome.
690 He had a voice as weak as a goat has.
He didn't have a beard and never would have.
His face was as smooth as if it had just been shaved.
I think he was a eunich or a woman.
But, as for his trade, there wasn't
such another pardoner from Berwick to Ware,
for in his luggage he had a pillow-case
which he said was Our Lady's veil.
He said he had a fragment of the sail
that Saint Peter had that time he went
700 on the sea, until Jesus Christ took him.
He had a brass cross set with stones
and he had some pigs' bones in a glass
but with these relics, when he found
a poor person scratching a living somewhere,
he got himself more money in just one day
than the Parson got in two months.

IV Analysis

A. Orthography

1. Manuscript A

Chaucer's spelling makes the language look more unfamiliar than it really is. This is even more so in the manuscript where there are a number of unfamiliar symbols and uses. In the transcription A and the modern version B, these have been altered to make the text less forbidding for a present-day reader.

(i) ⟨ẏ⟩ for ⟨i⟩

A dotted ⟨ẏ⟩ is used where ⟨i⟩ would appear today: *hẏm* (A669), *strẏke* (A676), *thẏnne* (A679). This was said to have originated to differentiate the vowel from surrounding consonants such as ⟨m⟩ and ⟨n⟩ whose tops were not joined in the script. If ⟨i⟩ had been used, many words would contain a series of downstrokes which would have been difficult to read.

(ii) ⟨þ⟩

This is an Old English symbol, thought to derive from runes. It was used for the voiced and voiceless sounds /ð/ and /θ/ which could not be easily represented in the Roman alphabet. Later, ⟨þ⟩ was replaced by ⟨th⟩ because of French influence. Here, ⟨þ⟩ only occurs in the abbreviated form for *that*: *þᵗ* (A677). ⟨th⟩ is used elsewhere: *ther* (A669), and it even appears in *that* (A671) at the beginning of a line.

(iii) ⟨u⟩ and ⟨v⟩

The distinction between ⟨u⟩ and ⟨v⟩ is not the modern one of vowel and consonant but is related to position. ⟨v⟩ occurs initially whether the sound is a vowel (A681: *vp*) or a consonant (A685: *vernycle*). ⟨u⟩ appears non-initially both as a consonant (A672: *loue*) and as a vowel (A698: *Iesu*).

(iv) ⟨I⟩ for ⟨J⟩

In the typed transcription of A, ⟨I⟩ is used for ⟨j⟩ and ⟨J⟩: *Iolitee* (A680), *Iesu* (A698). ⟨J⟩ did not occur in Old English. It was introduced by French scribes after the Norman Conquest, so was probably still relatively new at this stage.

(v)   Long ⟨ʃ⟩
Ordinary ⟨s⟩ occurs finally (A694: *his*) and initially (A690: *smothe*) but long ⟨ʃ⟩ is used in the middle of a word (A681: *truʃʃed*, A683: *diʃcheuelee*, A690: *ẏʃhaue*). Like ⟨u⟩ and ⟨v⟩, ⟨ʃ⟩ is positionally determined.

(vi)   Abbreviations
It is often claimed that words were abbreviated to justify the right-hand margin, but this explanation does not seem to apply here. In addition to *ƥ'*, abbreviations occur with ⟨er⟩, ⟨ur⟩ and ⟨ar⟩: *neûe* for *neuere* (A674), *Somonō* for *Somonour* (A673) and *pʃon* for *person* (A702). In some cases, the abbreviations show elision. *Pdoner* (A675) needs to have only two syllables, while *Pardoner* (A693) has three to keep the lines at ten syllables each.

(vii)   Punctuation
Punctuation is sparser in transcription A than in the modern version B:

    A672:   Ful loude he soong / com hyder loue to me
    B674:   Ful loude he soong 'Com hider, love, to me!'

The slant lines usually occur in the middle of lines rather than commas or full stops. They are probably an aid to reading aloud, as much poetry would have belonged to an oral tradition. Capital letters appear at the beginning of lines, although some are unusual (A672: *fful*, A697: *Peter*). Capitals are also used for proper nouns in the Hengwrt but not always in the Ellesmere manuscript (A671: *Court of Rome*, A697: *Seint Peter*). Sometimes they appear with common nouns (A688: *Goot*, A694: *Male*).

(viii)   Variant spellings
Since spelling wasn't standardised until after the beginning of

the modern period, it is not surprising that the Hengwrt manuscript contains different spellings of the same word (A677: *þᵗ*, A671: *that*, A676: *heeng*, A677: *henge* for 'hung'). There are even more variations between the Hengwrt and Ellesmere manuscripts:

	Hengwrt	*Ellesmere*
A699	cros (Germanic, Viking)	croys (French)
A678	his	hise
A701	foond	fond
A670	comper	compeer
A676	stryke	strike
A704	persoun ('parson')	person ('parson')
A702	person ('person')	persoun ('person')

2.   *Manuscript B*

(i)   *Final ⟨e⟩s*

Extra ⟨e⟩s occur on many words. Some are relics of Old English inflections. This is true of plurals and possessives, whose ⟨e⟩s were pronounced in the recording: *monthes* (B706), *stones* (B701), *pigges* (B702). Some ⟨e⟩s are variable, being pronounced only to ensure that there are ten syllables in the line, as in *sholde* (B691) and *trussed* (B683) but not in *sowed* (B687).

Some final ⟨e⟩s show spelling rules at work. *smothe* (B678) has a final ⟨e⟩, presumably to show that the vowel in the middle is a long /oː/, if not yet a long /uː/. Sometimes the final consonant is doubled and then an ⟨e⟩ added to show that the preceding vowel is short: *cappe* (B687), *hadde* (B677).

However, there are many final ⟨e⟩s on words whose inflections have probably disappeared: there is a distinct impression that literate people were so used to seeing these ⟨e⟩s in French or in older forms of English that they sprinkled them on words for effect. Again, the ⟨e⟩s do not seem to justify the line here. Examples include: *Oure* (B697), *wente* (B699), *loude* (B674), *nevere* (B691).

(ii) Doubling

Doubling also occurs with vowels. It seems to suggest a long vowel: /o:/ in *rood* (B671), *noon* (B682) and *hoot* (B689); /e:/ in *freend* (B672) and *compeer* (B672).

In contrast, some consonants which are doubled in Modern English aren't in this extract: *ful* (B674), *stif* (B675), *al* (B684).

(iii) Pronunciation

The recording showed that spelling and pronunciation were much closer in Late Middle English than they are today. Post-vocalic ⟨r⟩s were pronounced in *Pardoner* /pardɒnɛr/ (B671) and /x/ occurred for ⟨gh⟩ in *streight* /straɪxt/ (B673). Several spellings could reflect Chaucer's regional pronunciation, as, since there was no standard spelling, people tended to write the way they spoke. Some blurring of /a/ and /e/ seems to be at work, possibly as a result of the pronunciation of /æ/. ⟨e⟩s not ⟨a⟩s are used in *wex* (B677) and *flex* (B678). The opposite has happened with *overspradde* (B680) and *whan* (B699). *lond* (B704) suggests an /ɒ/ rather than an /a/ pronunciation. The ⟨d⟩ in *hider* (B674) shows an Old English form, while *an* before *hare* (B686) suggests the initial consonant has been dropped rather as in French words.

A number of words illustrate elision. This is a common speech feature in which a sound is omitted. In *shuldres* (B680) and *pilwe* (B696), the vowels have been omitted before ⟨r⟩ and ⟨w⟩ respectively. *fro* (B673) for 'from' is a Scandinavian form and *soun* (B676) for 'sound' is French, the extra ⟨d⟩ being added in the sixteenth century. *biforn* 'before' (B688) and *swiche* 'such' (B686) are examples of Old English forms with consonants ⟨n⟩ and ⟨w⟩ which have been elided in Modern English.

B. Vocabulary

1. Archaisms

It is often difficult to distinguish archaisms from rare or obsolete words. Archaisms are words which appear old fashioned or dated. Consequently, they are not used very much in Modern English. They often seem to be reserved for formal occasions or specialised use as in religious language. Examples include: B674: *hider* (*hither* 'here'), B675: *bar* ('bore'), B676: *trompe* (*trump(et)*), B679: *lokkes* (*locks* 'hair'), B700: *upon* ('on'), B704: *dwellinge* ('living'). B693 *trowe* (*trow* 'believe') is listed in the OED as archaic but is probably obsolete.

B680 *therewith* ('with it') also demonstrates an older pattern of word formation which was common. Here, an adverb is followed by a preposition. Similarly, *overspradde* (B680) would be more likely to be *spread over* nowadays with the preposition following the verb rather than occurring in a compound before it.

gelding (B693) is probably a more specialised term today, as horses are a less important part of life. It is rare and technical rather than archaic.

2. Obsolete words

Although much of the vocabulary in the extract seems strange, surprisingly little is totally obsolete today. Not many more than half a dozen words are obsolete today:

Word	Meaning	Last Quotation in OED
colpons (B681)	rats-tails	1548 with ⟨l⟩ spelling
bret (B689)	brim	1616
beer (B696)	case	Obsolete spelling. Modern spelling not until after 1600. Influenced by French *bière*. Now specialised as a 'movable stand for a corpse'.
hente (B700)	took	1651
latoun (B701)	brass	1890
gobet (B698)	fragment	Listed as rare and archaic but last quotation in which meaning is not also explained is 1648.

vernicle (B687)	a picture of Christ's face, as on St Veronica's handkerchief, worn by pilgrims	1853. Not called obsolete in OED, but so rare and specialised that it probably seems obsolete to the modern reader.

3. Semantic change

Most of the vocabulary is unusual because it has changed its meaning rather than because the form is totally unfamiliar. In addition, sometimes extra nuances are also present. Care must be taken, as it is easy to make a sensible translation with the modern equivalent and miss the true meaning.

gentil (B671) has more of the sense of 'nobility', 'courtesy' and 'charm' present in our meaning of *gentleman* rather than the 'mild in disposition' of our modern *gentle*. *stif* (B675) is now restricted to the meaning of 'rigid' rather than 'strong' or 'deep', although the whole expression 'bar to him a stif burdoun' may contain sexual innuendo. *burdoun* (B675) comes from French and means both 'bass accompaniment' and 'pilgrim's staff'. It was later confused with the Old English word *burden* because of its associations with 'heaviness'. Riding all *bare* (B685) does not mean 'completely naked' but 'bareheaded', which would have been unusual then. *glaringe* eyes (B686) are 'staring' or 'bulging' ones. A modern *compere* is someone who hosts a television show rather than a 'companion', although *peer* means 'someone of the same age or status', so the relationship between *compeer* (B672) and 'companion' can be easily seen.

Some words have slight differences in meaning. A *smal* voice (B690) is 'weak' in capacity. *soun* (B676) is more likely to be translated as 'noise' rather than 'sound'. *biforn* (B688) means 'in front of'. The modern *before* tends to be reserved for time.

late (B692) means 'just' and is used as an adverb, not an adjective. *save* (B685), from the French *sauf*, is a preposition, not a verb.

One of the most common ways that a word can change its

meaning is by narrowing. An example of narrowing can be seen in the word *walet* (B683). Nowadays, a *wallet* is small and is specifically used for carrying money. Then, it was used to carry all types of personal possessions – it can be equated with the modern 'saddlebag'. Similarly, *ounces* (B679) refers specifically to a small measure of weight and can't be used for hair hanging in small clumps. The homophone of *male* (B696), *mail*, is now used for the 'post'. Then, it could mean any sort of 'luggage'. *trussed* (B683) is more likely to refer today to people or fowl rather than to a hood being packed away in a bag.

The word *craft* (B694) could have some of the pejorative overtones it has today, being associated with 'cunning' as well as with 'trade'. On the other hand, *smothe* (B678) seems to have improved in meaning today. It does not have the unfavourable connotations of 'lankly' which it has in this Late Middle English extract.

Two words, *strike* (B678) and *jet* (B684), are familiar to the present-day reader but their respective meanings of 'hank' and 'fashion' seem removed from present-day meaning. *jet* is associated with the French for 'throw' or 'cast', while *strike* is like Modern English *streak*. With ingenuity, it is doubtless possible to trace a link in meaning down to the present day.

4. French words

It has been estimated that over 10 000 French words were adopted into the English language during the 200 years following the Norman Conquest. Chaucer's English therefore contains a large number of French words which would not have been in the English language if Chaucer had written several centuries earlier. Examples of these include: *gentil* (B671), *Pardoner* (B671), *compeer* (B672), *court* (B673), *Somonour* (B675), *jolitee* (B682), *walet* (B683), *jet* (B684), *pardoun* (B689), *voys* (B690), *crois* (B701) and *dischevelee* (B685), which also shows French morphology and French spelling with ⟨ch⟩. Some of these French words are not in common use today: *burdoun* (B675), *colpons* (B681), *vernicle* (B687), *latoun* (B701). This suggests that French influence was stronger in the fourteenth century than it is today.

5. *Idiom*

Many of the expressions are not totally idiomatic Modern English. *a crois of latoun* (B701) is more likely to have the adjective in front of the noun nowadays and be described as a 'brass cross'. The Pardoner is seen as being *of Rouncivale* (B672) rather than 'from Rouncivale'. The *of* seems to be a direct translation of the French *de*. The same seems to have happened in *the court of Rome* (B673). It could be that some of the phraseology, as well as the individual vocabulary items, has also been influenced by French.

C. *Grammar*

As Old English became Modern English, the language gradually changed from a synthetic language with inflections and less strict word order to a more analytic language with few grammatical endings and a more rigid word order. This Chaucerian extract illustrates a position half-way between Old and Modern English. It has more inflections but a less rigid word order than Modern English.

1. *Word order*

The modern translation of Manuscript C generally has a subject, predicator, object/complement, adverbial word order, SP(O/C) (A). The Late Middle English extract departs from this pattern in several respects. In part, this could be to maintain the rhyming couplets and the iambic rhythm of the line.

(i) *Inversion of subject and predicator*

An example of freer word order can be seen in the frequent inversion of subject and predicator. This is often accompanied by movement of the object (B691, B687, B686) or adverbial (B679) to an initial thematic position in the sentence:

```
               O          P          S
   B691:   (No berd) (hadde) (he)

               S       P           O
   C691:   (He) (didn't have) (a beard)
```

```
          O         P        S      P     · A
B687:   (A vernicle) (hadde) (he) (sowed) (upon his cappe)
          S      P        O          A
C687:   (He) (had sewn) (a Veronica) (on to his cap)

          O                   P       S     A
B686:   (Swich glaringe eyen) (hadde) (he) (as an hare)
          S    P    O              A
C686:   (He) (had) (such staring eyes) (like a hare)

          A         P       S
B679:   (By ounces) (henge) (his lokkes that he hadde)
          S               P       A
C679:   (What hair he had) (hung) (in rats-tails)
```

Inversion also seems to occur with negatives:

```
               P     S       C
B695:       Ne (was) (ther) (swich another pardoner)
               S      P        C
C694–5:   (there) (wasn't) (such another pardoner)
```

In Modern English, inversion of subject and predicator tends to occur mainly in interrogatives.

(ii)   Thematic adverbials
Adverbials occur initially quite frequently without subject and predicator inversion. A more usual position in Modern English, at least in prose, is at the end of a sentence.

```
          A          S    P        O
B674:   (Ful loude) (he) (soong) ('Com hider, love, to me!')
          S    P     O                            A
C674:   (He) (sang) ('Come hither, love, to me!') (very loudly)

            A       S   P
B681:   But (thinne) (it) (lay)
```

```
        S    P    A
C681:  but (it) (lay) (thinly)
```

(iii)   Object placement
In addition to thematic objects, there are a couple of unusual
examples of object placement. In B680, the object *his shuldres*
is placed between the subject, *he*, and the predicator, *overspradde*. The same has happened with *him* in B700.

```
           A        S    O              P
B680:  And (therwith) (he) (his shuldres) (overspradde)
           S    P         O              A
C680:  And (he) (covered) (his shoulders) (with it)
           S              O    P
B700:  ... til (Jhesu Crist) (him) (hente)
           S              P    O
C700:  ... until (Jesus Christ) (took) him
```

2.   Verbs
The verb is the word class which, in this extract, seems to show
the biggest difference in terms of inflections and forms.

(i)   Present tense (e)th endings
The third person singular present forms do not have *-s* endings
but retain an older *(e)th* inflection: *dooth* (B678), *does* (C678);
hath (B690), *has* (C690). The *-s* ending later spread from the
North.

(ii)   Past forms
The biggest difference in past forms concerns strong and weak
verbs. Strong verbs change their vowels in the past tense, while
weak verbs add *-ed*. The general movement from Old English
to Modern English has been a trend towards weak *-ed* endings.
It is surprising therefore that this Chaucer extract shows the
reverse. It contains several verbs with weak *-ed* endings whose
equivalent modern forms have retained the strong forms by
changing the vowel or by using the *-n* form in the past
participle: *wered* 'wore' (B682); *sowed* (B687), *sewn* (C687).

In a number of other places, *-en* seems to be a typical past participle ending: *was comen* (B673), *had come* (C673); *comen* (B689), *having come* (C689). The perfect auxiliary HAVE does not appear here with the intransitive verb *come*. However, it does occur with transitive verbs such as *sew*:

B687:   A vernicle *hadde* he sowed upon his cappe

C687:   He *had* sewn a Veronica on to his cap

A number of other strong verbs seem to have different vowels in their past forms in the Chaucer extract. In some cases, this could be because of Chaucer's regional accent or because of subsequent sound changes (for example, B671: *rood*, C671: *rode*). In other instances, it is likely that the verbs were categorised differently grammatically (for example, B705 *gat* has ⟨a⟩ in the middle like the past of *drank*, not ⟨o⟩ as in C705 *got*). Other examples of strong verbs with different vowels from Modern English include: B674: *soong*, C674: *sang*; B675: *bar*, 'bore'; B678: *heeng*, C678: *hung*.

Two interesting past participles are *dischevelee* (B685), with a French past participle ending, and *shave* (B692), which in the modern version B has no ending at all. A reasonable translation of B692 is with a past perfect passive:

B692:   As smothe it was as it *were* late *shave*

C692:   His face was as smooth as if it *had* just *been shaved*

The *were* seems to convey past, perfect and passive, as well as some sort of subjunctive condition suggested by *if*. The sentence suggests that the auxiliary system was not as well developed in Middle English as it is today. The Hengwrt manuscript has an alternative spelling of *shave* as *ẏſhaue* (A690) with the old past participle prefix *y*. This is probably a preferable reading, as not only does it mark *shave* as a past participle, but it also means that the line has the regular number of ten syllables.

In B693, *were*, which in Modern English tends to be a plural verb, is used for the subjunctive with a singular subject after the verb *trowe*, which conveys speculation:

B693:   I trowe he *were* a gelding or a mare

C693:   I think he *was* a eunich or a woman

The modal *sholde* in B691 is used with a third person subject. Nowadays, *should* tends to convey duty and occurs in conditional uses mainly with a first person subject. *would* is used in C691:

B691:   No berd hadde he, ne nevere *sholde* have

C691:   He didn't have a beard and never *would* have

(iii)   Impersonal uses

It is tempting to translate *Him thoughte* (B684) as 'he thought'. However, in the Chaucer extract, it retains a sense of an earlier impersonal use in which *him* was an indirect object or dative form meaning 'to him', while *thoughte* was an impersonal verb rather like the Modern English *it seemed*. A better translation of B684 therefore is 'It seemed to him that . . .'. This seems more sarcastic than 'he thought'.

3.   Negatives

The common way of showing a negative in the older extract is by the use of *ne* before the verb:

B695:   *Ne* was ther swich another pardoner

C694–5:   there was*n't* such another pardoner

Nowadays, an *n't* is attached to the end of an auxiliary verb, and if there is no auxiliary verb present, a *do* carrier verb is introduced. This is probably to make the negative more obvious. Because negatives are unstressed, they tend to become weakened and lost, so have to be reinforced by another form. This is presumably what happened to the *ne* negative used by Chaucer which was then reinforced by *not* (from *na whit*), after the verb. In Modern English, *not* has become weakened to *n't*, so a carrier verb has been introduced. It will be interesting to see if, in the future, further negative weakening followed by reinforcement takes place.

Chaucer also seems to reinforce the negative by using negative forms such as *noon*, as in B682, with positive verbs rather than an indefinite *a* or *any* with a negative verb, as in C682:

> B682:   But hood, for jolitee, wered he *noon*
>
> C682:   He did*n't* wear *any* hood in order to be festive

He also reinforces the negative by placing it initially and using several in a line, as in B691:

> B691:   *No* berd hadde he, *ne nevere* sholde have
>
> C691:   He did*n't* have a beard and *never* would have
>   (or: would *never* have one)

4. *Nouns*

Plurals and possessives have -*s* endings like Modern English but are preceded by an ⟨e⟩: *pigges* (B702), *pigs'* or *pig's* (C702); *relikes* (B703), *relics* (C703). However, there are a couple of exceptions: *eyen* (B686), *eyes* (C686); *Lady* (B697), *Lady's* (C697). *eyen* is an older -*en* plural and *Lady* an older possessive form which by Middle English had a zero ending. There are only a few remnants of -*en* plurals left today: *oxen*, *children* and *brethren*.

There are one or two differences in pronouns. The reflexive in B705 is *him* rather than *himself*:

> B705:   Upon a day he gat *him* moore moneye . . .
>
> C705:   he got *himself* more money in just one day . . .

Which that (B697) is used as a kind of double relative pronoun. In Modern English, either *which* or *that* would be used but not both. The Middle English usage is rather reminiscent of the French pattern *ce qui/que*:

B696–7: . . . he hadde a pilwe beer,
Which *that* he seyde was Oure Lady veil

C696–7: . . . he had a pillow-case
which he said was Our Lady's veil

The final difference in nouns concerns the placement of an adjective in one of the noun phrases. In B706, *tweye* is placed after the noun *monthes* rather than before it, as it would be in Modern English. The pattern used in the older extract is again typical of French:

B706: . . . in monthes *tweye*

C706: . . . in *two* months

5. *Adjectives as adverbs*

As in many modern dialects, this Middle English extract has a number of examples of adverbs without any -*ly* type of ending:

B674: Ful *loude* he soong 'Com hider, love, to me!'

C674: He sang 'Come hither, love, to me!' very *loudly*

B681: But *thinne* it lay

C681: but it lay *thinly*

It will also be noticed that *ful* is used as an intensifier *very* in B674.

V Evaluation

When the project was first started, I was afraid that there would not be enough material to discuss in such a short extract. With more extensive research, I discovered that there was actually too much for the word limit. Consequently, I had to undertake a painful pruning of the first draft and limit myself to the main points.

I was surprised at the extent of the differences in spelling between the Manuscript A and the modern version B. The Late

Middle English extract actually contained more words which are spelt differently from Modern English than are spelt the same. Even the modern version B has many differences from Modern English. The unfamiliar appearance explains part of the difficulty of the text. I was also surprised at the variant spellings, at the different spelling rules which are at work in the Chaucerian extract, and at how important the position is to the symbols used in the Manuscript A. My study of spelling has helped me to understand that the apparently inconsistent nature of present-day spelling is because it was based on earlier pronunciation.

As far as vocabulary is concerned, my major discovery was that not many words were totally unfamiliar, but care had to be taken because familiar words might have a slightly different meaning. Not unexpected was the amount of French influence on the lexis, but there also seemed to be French influence on phraseology, much of which was not totally idiomatic Modern English. There seemed little evidence of Scandinavian influence, considering that the Vikings started arriving in the eighth and ninth centuries. This is probably because the text is Southern rather than Northern.

With regard to grammar, there were differences in nearly all aspects, with the retention of inflections on verbs and nouns, and a freer word order than in Modern English. However, some of the differences are no doubt because of the metrical nature of the extract and most would not be unknown to a modern reader acquainted with poetry or older literature, or with conservative varieties of English used in religion and law.

Overall, I was surprised at the amount of information that I unearthed and enjoyed the research for this project. I have learnt a lot about language change and have also learnt to select, summarise and balance the main points of a longer piece of work.

VI Bibliography

Background reading

Baugh, A.C. and Cable, T. (1951) *A History of the English Language* London and New York: Routledge and Kegan Paul

The Compact Edition of the Oxford English Dictionary (1971) Oxford: Clarendon

Robinson, F.A. (1974) *The Complete Works of Geoffrey Chaucer* London: OUP

Ruggiers, Paul G. (ed.) (1979) *The Canterbury Tales: A Facsimile and Transcription of the Hengwrt Manuscript with Variants from the Ellesmere Manuscript* Folkstone, Kent: Wm Dawson & Sons Ltd

Winny, J. (ed.) (1976) *The General Prologue to the Canterbury Tales* Cambridge: CUP

16
Conclusion

Now that you have completed your language project, you should find that not only do you have an increased knowledge about the way language works, but that you are also able to apply this knowledge yourself to pieces of language that you have not seen before.

You should also have acquired skills and concepts which are useful generally. For example, the study has been independent and sustained. It has involved analysis and probably the realisation that various interpretations of one situation can be equally valid.

During the study, your skim reading and reference skills should have improved, as you scanned a wide range of books for background information. In addition, close reading was involved – for instance, in the examination of your material.

As far as writing is concerned, your note-taking, drafting and report writing skills should now be better. Completing your polished version, possibly using other graphical methods of communication, should have underlined the importance of neat and appropriate presentation and layout. You may also have gained experience in the use of information technology, if you used a word processor in the drafting and production of your project.

If you have used spoken material, close listening will have been involved as you transcribed your tape. The investigation will probably also have included speaking and listening skills, as you discussed your topic with your teacher or lecturer, or other interested parties. Finally, you might like to consider enhancing your oral work even further by planning a spoken presentation of your findings to a chosen group either now or some time in the future.

Bibliography

Brown, R. (1973) *A First Language: The Early Stages* London: Allen and Unwin

Carter, R. (1987) *Vocabulary* London: Allen and Unwin

Crystal, D. and Davy, D. (1969) *Investigating English Style* London: Longman

Crystal, D. (1976) *Child Language, Learning and Linguistics* London: Arnold

de Villiers, P.A. and de Villiers, J.G. (1979) *Early Language* London: Fontana

Dubin, F. (1987) 'Answering Machines' in *English Today* **10**. 28–30

Freeborn, D. with Langford, D. and French, P. (1986) *Varieties of English: An Introduction to the Study of Language* Basingstoke: Macmillan

Freeborn, D. (1987) *A Course Book in English Grammar* Basingstoke: Macmillan

Fromkin, V. and Rodman, R. (1983) 3rd edn *An Introduction to Language* New York: Holt-Saunders

Gimson, A.C. (1980) 3rd edn *An Introduction to the Pronunciation of English* London: Edward Arnold

Hughes, A. and Trudgill, P. (1979) *English Accents and Dialects: A Guide to Social and Regional Varieties of British English* London: Edward Arnold

Ingram, D. (1986) 'Phonological patterns in the speech of young children' in Fletcher, P. and Garman, H. (eds) *Language Acquisition* Cambridge: CUP

McCrum, R. (1987) *The Story of English* London: Faber

McTear, M.F. (1985) *Children's Conversation* Oxford: Basil Blackwell

O'Donnell, W.R. and Todd, L. (1980) *Variety in Contemporary English* London: Allen and Unwin

The Oxford English Dictionary (1989) 2nd edn Oxford: Clarendon

The Compact Edition of the Oxford English Dictionary (1971) Oxford: Clarendon

Palmer, F. (1981) 2nd edn *Semantics* Cambridge: CUP

Pellowe, J. (1976) *Phonology and Phonetics Manual* Department of English Language, University of Newcastle upon Tyne

Quirk, R. and Greenbaum, S. (1973) *A University Grammar of English* London: Longman

Quirk, R., Greenbaum, S., Leech, G. and Svartvik, J. (1985) *A Comprehensive Grammar of the English Language* London: Longman

Stern, G. (1965) 2nd edn *Meaning and Change of Meaning* London: Greenwood Press

Tinkel, A.J. (1988) *Explorations in Language* Cambridge: CUP

Trudgill, P. and Hannah, J. (1985) 2nd edn *International English: A Guide to Varieties of Standard English* London: Edward Arnold

Wardhaugh, R. (1985) *How Conversation Works* Oxford: Blackwell

West, M. (1953) *A General Service List of English Words* London: Longman

Young, David J. (1984) *Introducing English Grammar* London: Hutchinson

Index